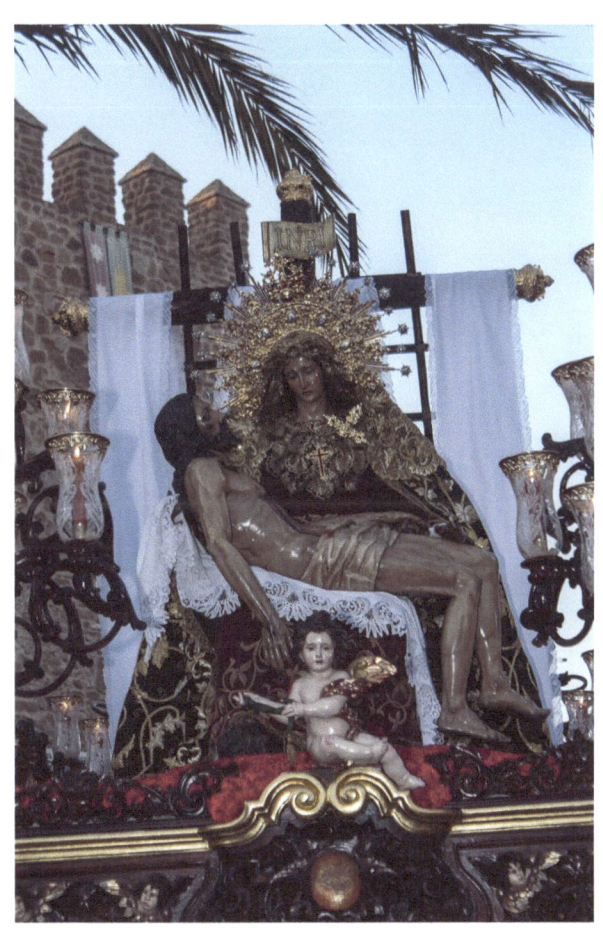

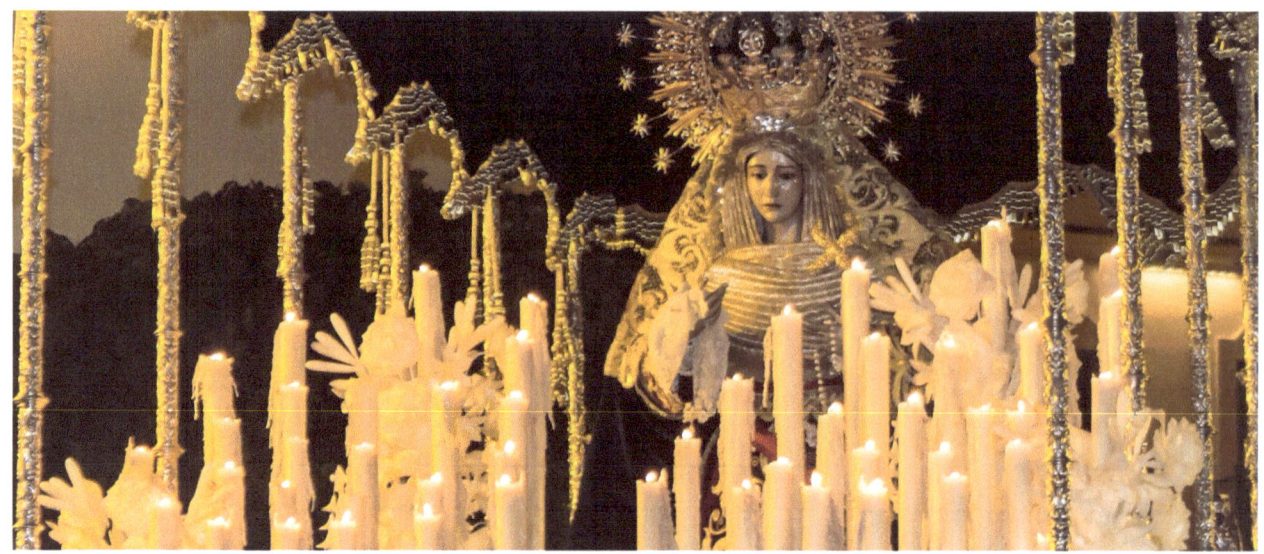

I would like to thank the following people for their invaluable contribution to this book;

Lynn Loman
Pastor Keith Swanson
Milagros Sanchez Leveque
Elena Gross
Alfonso de Orléans-Borbón
David Frasier-Luckie
The Tourist Information Office of Rota, Spain
Shirley DeMarr

Introduction

Spain is a highly thought of travel destination for many. Beautiful beaches, outstanding food, and world renowned wine along with idyllic weather draw many tourists. The history, architecture, and art make it irresistible to many more. But you may not think of it as a place to go for Holy Week. Spain celebrates Holy Week in a way that pays homage to how we used to communicate 500 years ago and it certainly brought new meaning to how I view penance and the value it can bring to my life. This vestige of Christianity, celebrated throughout most of the Hispanic world, stimulated me mentally, emotionally, and spiritually in ways I would have never expected.

Religious brotherhoods perform penance processions through the streets of virtually every village, town, and city in Spain during the final week of Lent (the week before Easter). The practice dates back to the 1500s when the Catholic Church decided to present the story of the final week of Christ's life, death, and resurrection in a way that a 16th century commoner could understand - visually.

Capturing Holy Week photographically recently became a passion of mine that I just couldn't shake off. The spectacle, pageantry, and outward display of devotion were overpowering temptations for me. The thought of capturing the intrinsic properties of these reverent ceremonies within the confining walls of two dimensional media has become much more than just a challenge for me. It has become an obsession in how to say the same old thing in a fresh and interesting way. My tools are shape, form, and color within a frame while my message has to be one of emotional and spiritual connection that transcends human barriers.

How do I show penitence, contrition, or sorrow within a picture and still awaken the viewers desire to dig deeper? How do I convey the pain that Holy Week echos while seizing the feeling of ultimate salvation that it represents? How do I spark the non-believers interest and empathy? And what is the spiritual journey for me? These are but a few of the questions that have mystified me since I started this project.

While I do not set out to make this a classical travel guide, I realize that context dictates that I pay heed to some of those conventions. My primary purpose is to share a unique experience with the uninitiated or give a record to those who have experienced it. Perhaps it will motivate you to go and experience it yourself or give you deeper understanding of your own faith. I do not know ... nor is there a need for me to know.

I chose to go to the Andalusian Province of Cadiz primarily because of my familiarity with the area. I also chose small villages over the larger more famous processions as I wanted to capture an experience focused more on the events of 2000 years ago than on a contemporary event which has to consider great legions of observers and tourists.

I was quite pleased with these decisions as it led to a much more intimate experience than could have possibly been achieved in Seville or Málaga. But if you are thinking of going, these two places must be on your list of places to consider.

I chose to stay in the village of Rota on the Atlantic coast. A village I am intimately familiar with as the Navy afforded me the opportunity to live there for several years during my service. We stayed at the Hotel Playa de la Luz, an older 4 star hotel right on the Atlantic Ocean that is well maintained. There are numerous accommodations to choose from in the area ranging from hostel to modern 5 star luxury hotel and, as of this writing, for quite reasonable prices.

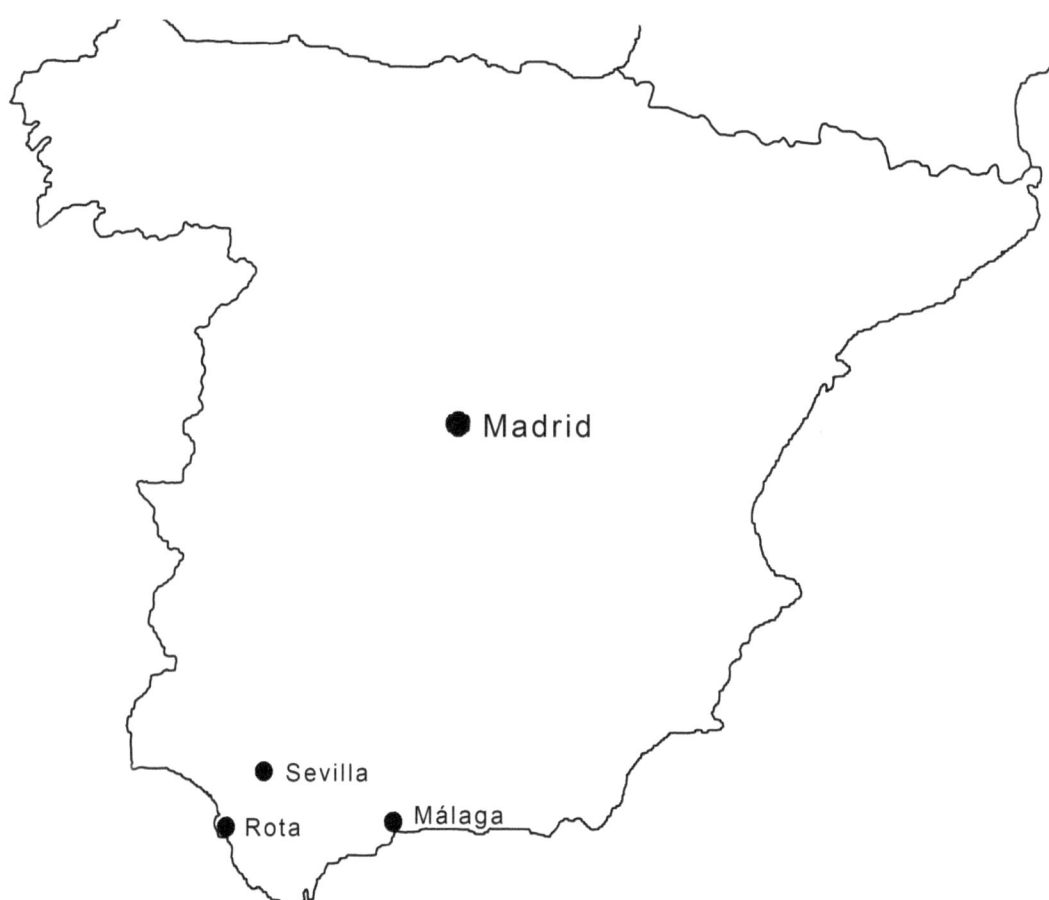

From the map above you can see that Rota is on the Atlantic coast and about 75 miles from Seville, 160 miles from Málaga, and about 400 miles from Madrid. Portugal is not shown on this map.

I should note that I did attend larger processions on Tuesday and Wednesday in El Puerto de Santa Maria and Jerez de la Frontera respectively (both are within 25 miles of Rota). Due to the help of friends, I had special access to these processions that allowed the intimate photography that I needed for this book to even come close to communicating the experience of being there.

English is widely spoken in Spain especially by those working in the tourist/service industry. In fact, in the larger coastal cities in the south where tourism is a big industry, there are areas where you might think that English is the first language. But to help surpass language barriers, one of the things most restaurants do is to have a reasonably high quality picture of each of their dishes. So, as many tourist do, you can chose by what visually appeals to you.

One thing that doing this book has shown me is that I am woefully inadequate at putting into words the emotions I am trying to convey. I am quite pleased with the photography in that it fulfills the context and emotion quite well. As is necessary in a project of this nature, some of the photography records events while some of it is truly fine art. And as is the case with things like art, the vast majority is a record of events. But please forgive my clumsy fumbling with the English language. If this book has any success what so ever I promise to use a professional editor on future updates!

Christianity in Spain

To understand Spain and its religious affinity, one must study its history and geography first of which the following only scratches the surface but I believe it gives an overall general flavor of the Spanish spiritual personality.

Most of Spain accepted Christianity while still part of the Roman Empire. After the demise of Rome, Moorish (North African) Muslims invaded Spain through Morocco in the 700s and Islam dominated most of the peninsula. A slow Christian reconquest took centuries and by 1492, with the fall of Grenada, the Moors and Muslim rule was for all practical purposes no longer a factor.

Imperial Spain began with the Renaissance New Monarchs Isabella and Ferdinand centralizing power and the word España becoming a common name for the area. With Christopher Columbus' discovery of the new world and the resulting expansion of trade routes, knowledge, agriculture, etc, now referred to as the Spanish Golden Age, Spain became a true world power.

The Protestant Reformation movement and its schism with the Catholic Church forced Spain into ever expanding military conflicts throughout Europe and the Mediterranean. This along with the plague caused an overall gradual decline of influence beginning in the latter half of the 17th century.

In 1851 Catholicism became the state religion and remained as such until 1931 when the secular constitution of the Second Spanish Republic threatened the church's leadership in Spain. This caused the church to support Francisco Franco during the Civil War.

During the Franco regime, the Catholic church was the only religion in Spain to have legal status. In order to be a Civil Servant during this period you had to be Catholic. Some official jobs even required a, "Good behavior" statement from a priest. The Second Vatican Council provided more rights to other religions in Spain in 1965.

After the death of Franco in 1975, King Juan Carlos de Borbón abdicated his right to name Bishops in 1976 and a gradual separation of church and state ensued.

Presently, about 70% of Spaniards are Catholic.

Semana Santa an Overview

Holy Week in Spain is the annual observance of the Passion of Jesus Christ celebrated by Catholic Cofridias and Hermandades(religious brotherhoods and sister-
hoods) who perform penance processions in the streets of nearly every Spanish city,
town, or village. It takes place the final week of Lent (the seven days before Easter).
Spain is renowned for its Semana Santa (Holy Week) celebrations and they date
from medieval times.

As a general rule, Semana Santa is a solemn and sombre occasion in the north
while the Andalusian region is known for its more glamorous celebrations. All Processions have numerous participants called Nazarenos dressed in penitent robes
and wear hoods with conical tips called a Capirote. The Nazarenos typically carry
processional candles, chains, or wooden crosses. Many walk the streets all night
long barefoot.

Many Americans, when first seeing a Nazareno, relate the penitent costume to the
Ku Klux Klan - that could not be further from the truth. The robe and Capirote pre-
date the KKK by hundreds of years and their purpose is significantly different; the
KKK used them to intimidate while disguising their identity - the penitent participating in a Procession in Spain wears his Capirote to ensure his penance is done anonymously. The conical tipped hat is a symbol of the ascension to heaven.

The most incredible part of these Procession for me are the huge floats, called
Pasos in Spanish, portraying scenes from the gospel with elaborate, life size sculptures of Jesus Christ, the Virgin Mary, or other scenes from the final week of Jesus'
life on Earth. The workmanship on these sculptures are absolutely astounding and
many are centuries old. These Pasos, weighing as much as two or three tons, are
carried about the streets by dozens of porters, called Costaleros. Often the Costaleros are hidden beneath the Paso so that it appears to float over the street.

The Costaleros wear a sack like cloth over their necks to soften the burden of the
float. In fact the name "Costalero" comes from the word "Costal" meaning a sack or a
direct translation would be something like a "sack man". The floats are built and
maintained by Brotherhoods who make up the Nazarenos leading the float through
the streets.

All of the Processions I attended had a Marching Band bringing up the rear of the
Procession playing funeral marches, hymns, or "marchas" (a rhythmic cadence).

A Saeta, performed by a Saetero (Saeta singer), is a revered form of religious song
sung in a flamenco tradition evoking strong emotions and is normally addressed to
one of the floats of Jesus or Mary. It is legend that the mournful power of the Procession would move some one to spontaneously burst into song. Now all Saetas are
well planned ahead of time and use professionals singers. The one Saeta that I
stayed to listen to was a very powerful moment with the float, Nazarenos, and assembled crowd making it a dreamlike scene.

Domingo de Ramos (Palm Sunday), Rota, Spain

Palm Sunday was the shortest duration of all the Holy Week Processions lasting only four hours. But after four hours of carrying 25 lbs of camera equipment, I was starting to get a clue about penance and what the penitent was trying to achieve.

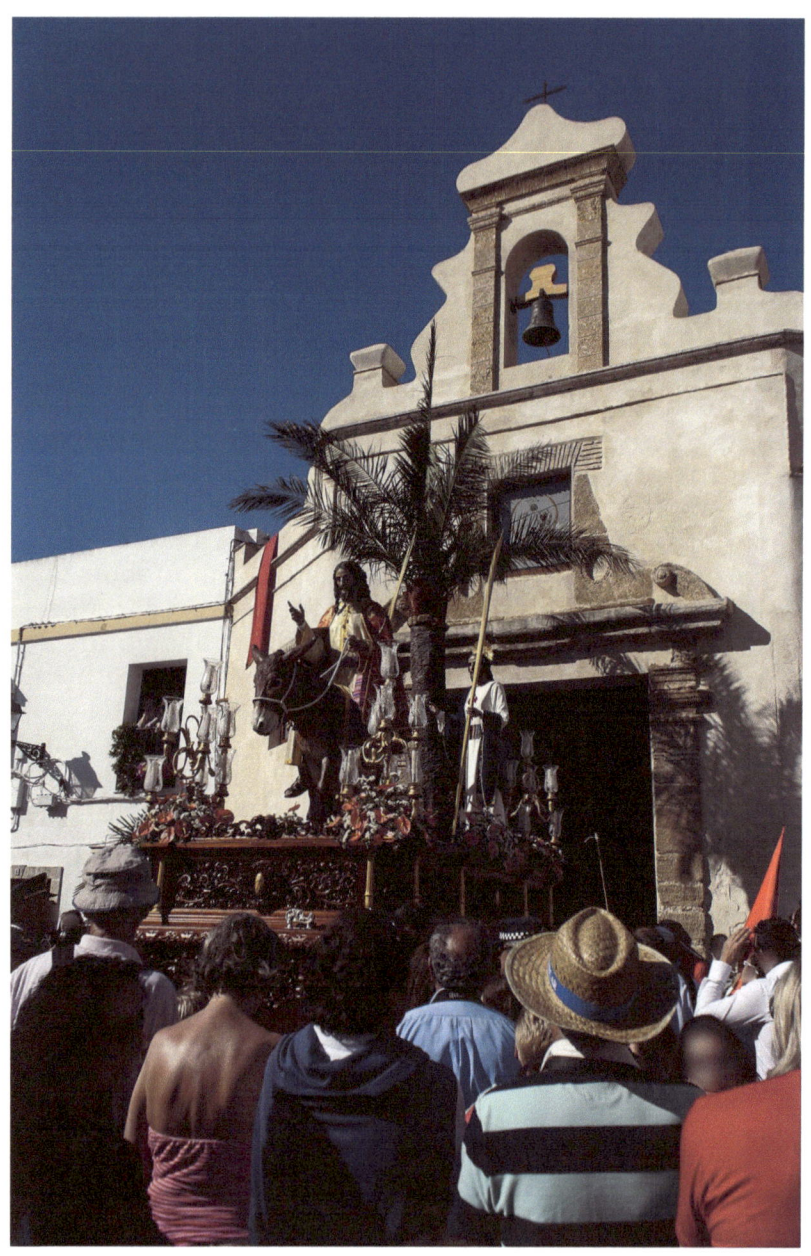

The Float of Jesus' Triumphal Entry into Jerusalem leaving the Capilla de San Roque (Chapel of San Roque). Some assembly is required. The palm behind Jesus is in a lowered position and once they get out of the Chapel, they raise it to the shown position.

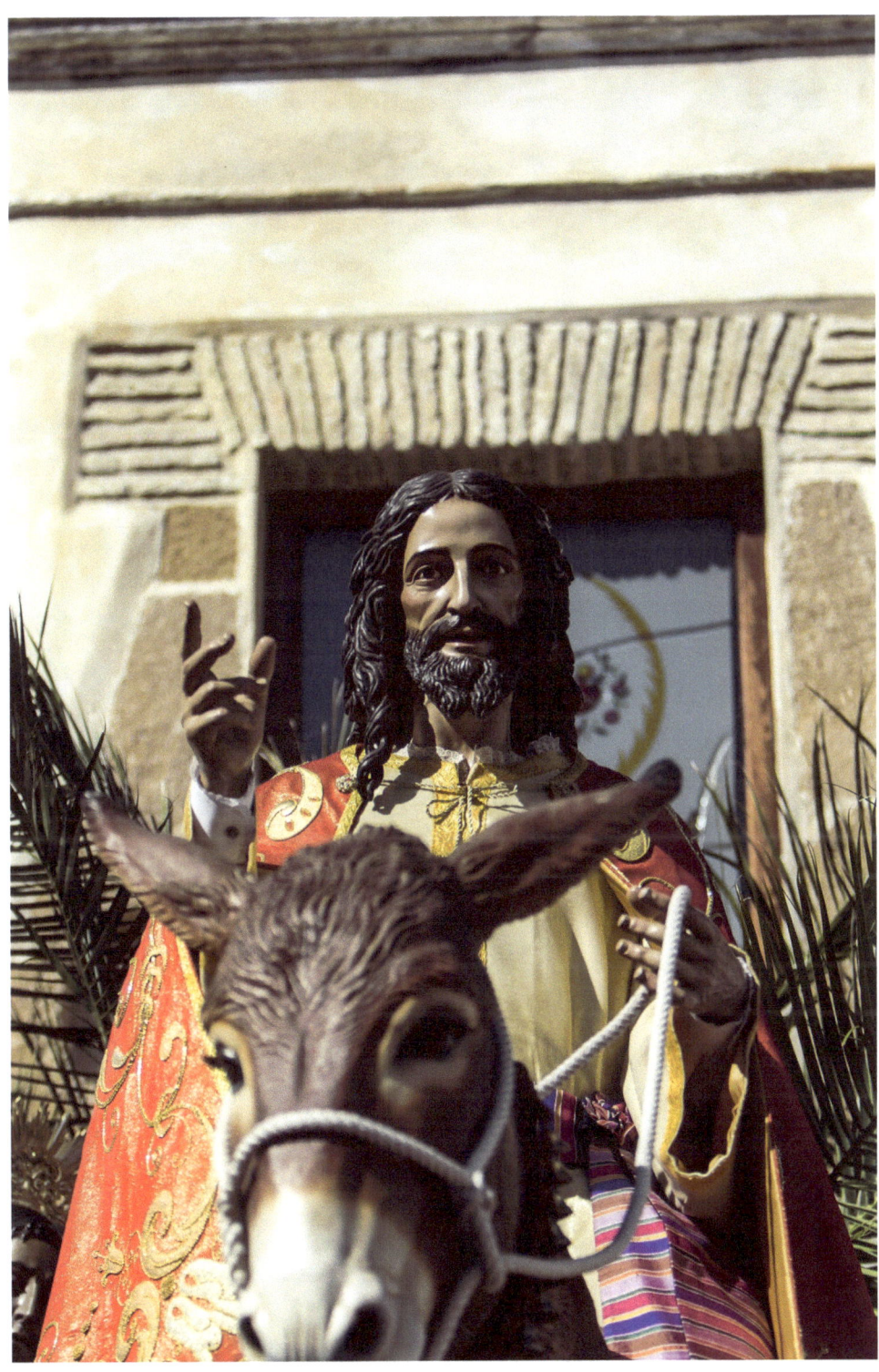

Here is a close up of Jesus showing the incredible detail of this wood carving and the craftsmanship that goes into them. Note that the palm in this shot is in the lowered position. Once the float has exited the Church the Costaleros set the float down on its feet so they can raise the object, in this case the palm, to its proper position.

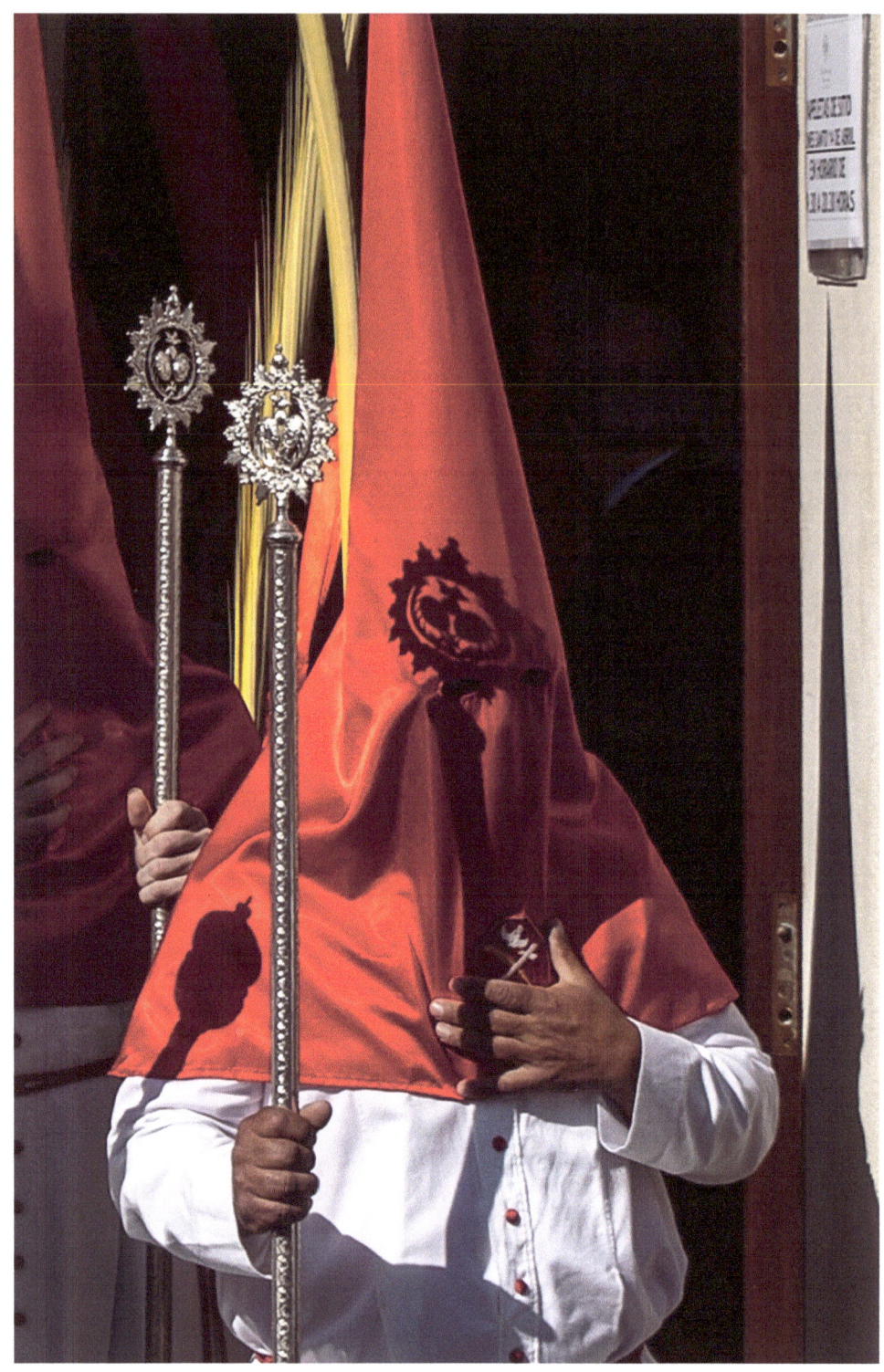

Penitent in traditional Robe and Capirote. To say this project was a study in symbolism is an understatement and I was especially taken by the shadow of the staff on his head in this picture. There is a hint as to the difficulty of wearing a Capirote. Because they are so tall they don't typically stay in place and the eye holes are limiting vision making walking over cobblestone streets, transiting curbs, and passing over sewer gratings precarious.

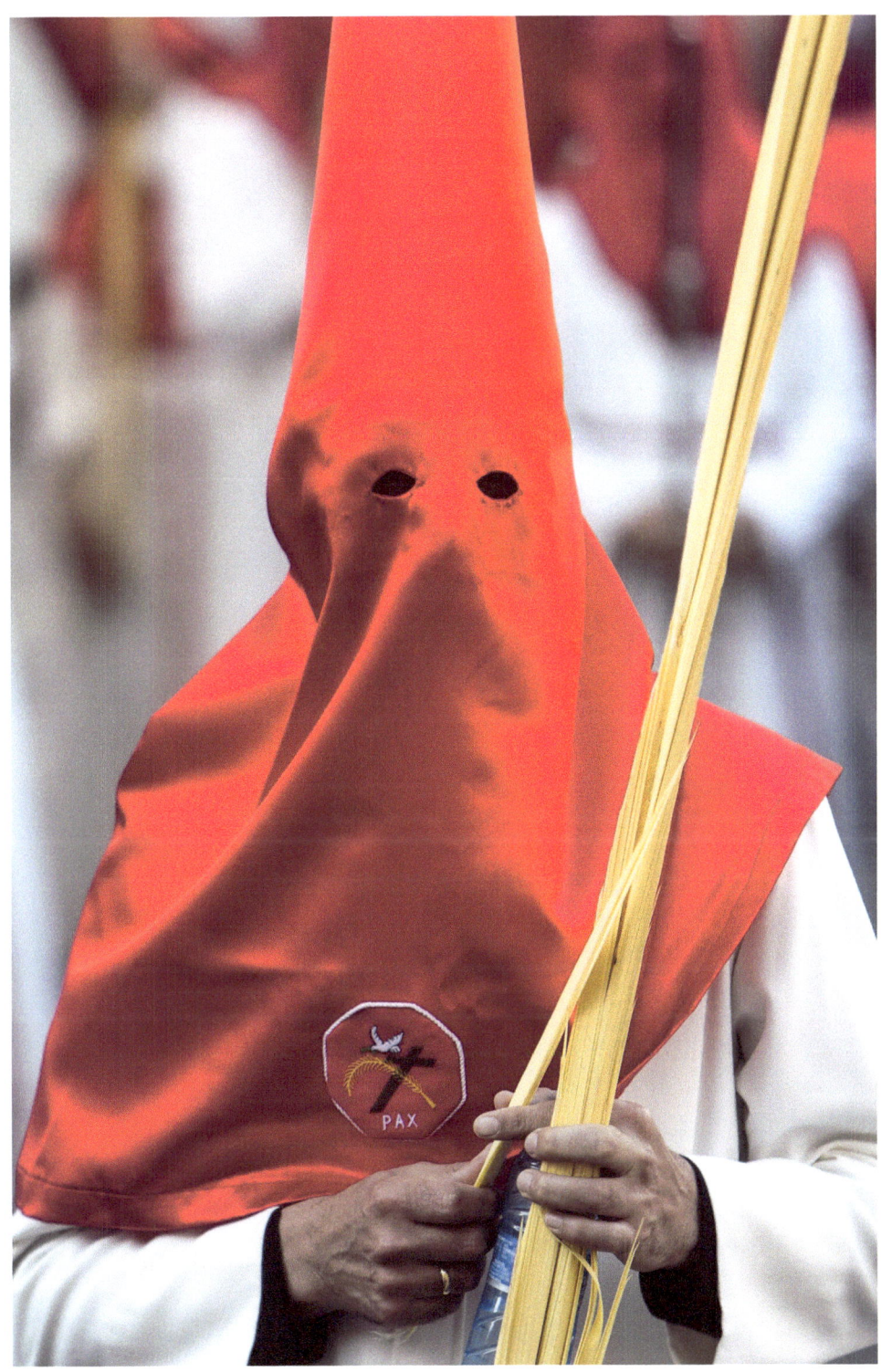

From the beginning I felt the challenge of this project was how to fully capture the expression of these ceremonies. I made the decision early on in the project to not reveal anyone's identity so I knew I would be depending heavily upon hands and eyes to explicitly state the message. While the eyes here are far too small to truly express anything, I just love how the penitents hands interlace with the palm leaves weaving a web like the juxtaposition of expectation at Jesus' arrival in Jerusalem.

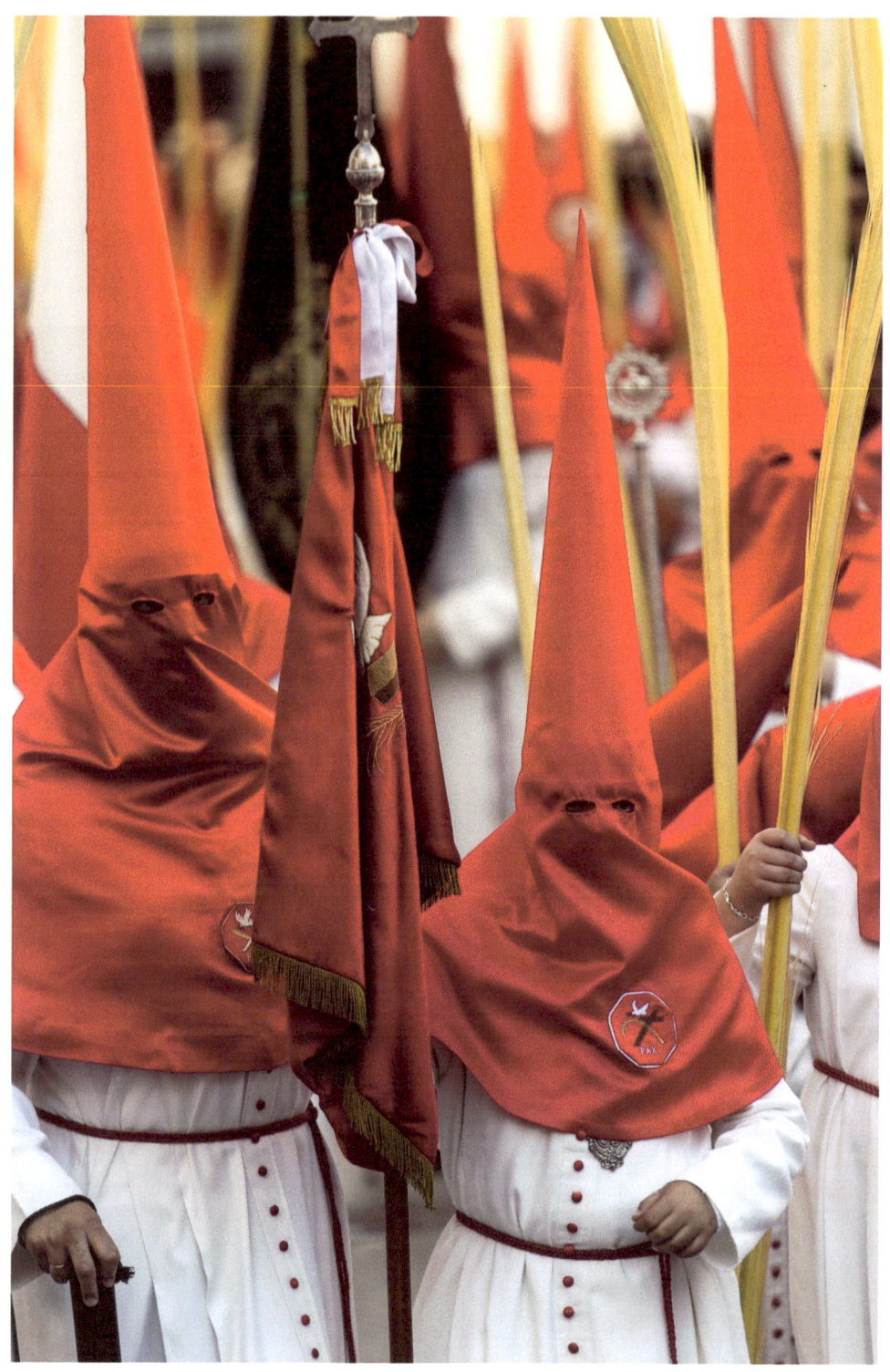

   A seemingly endless line of Penitents marching with their palms in search of abso-
lution. While this was the shortest duration of all the scheduled Processions it certainly seemed to go on and on. I was really taken aback by the number of participants for such a small village.

Lunes Santo (Holy Monday), Rota, Spain

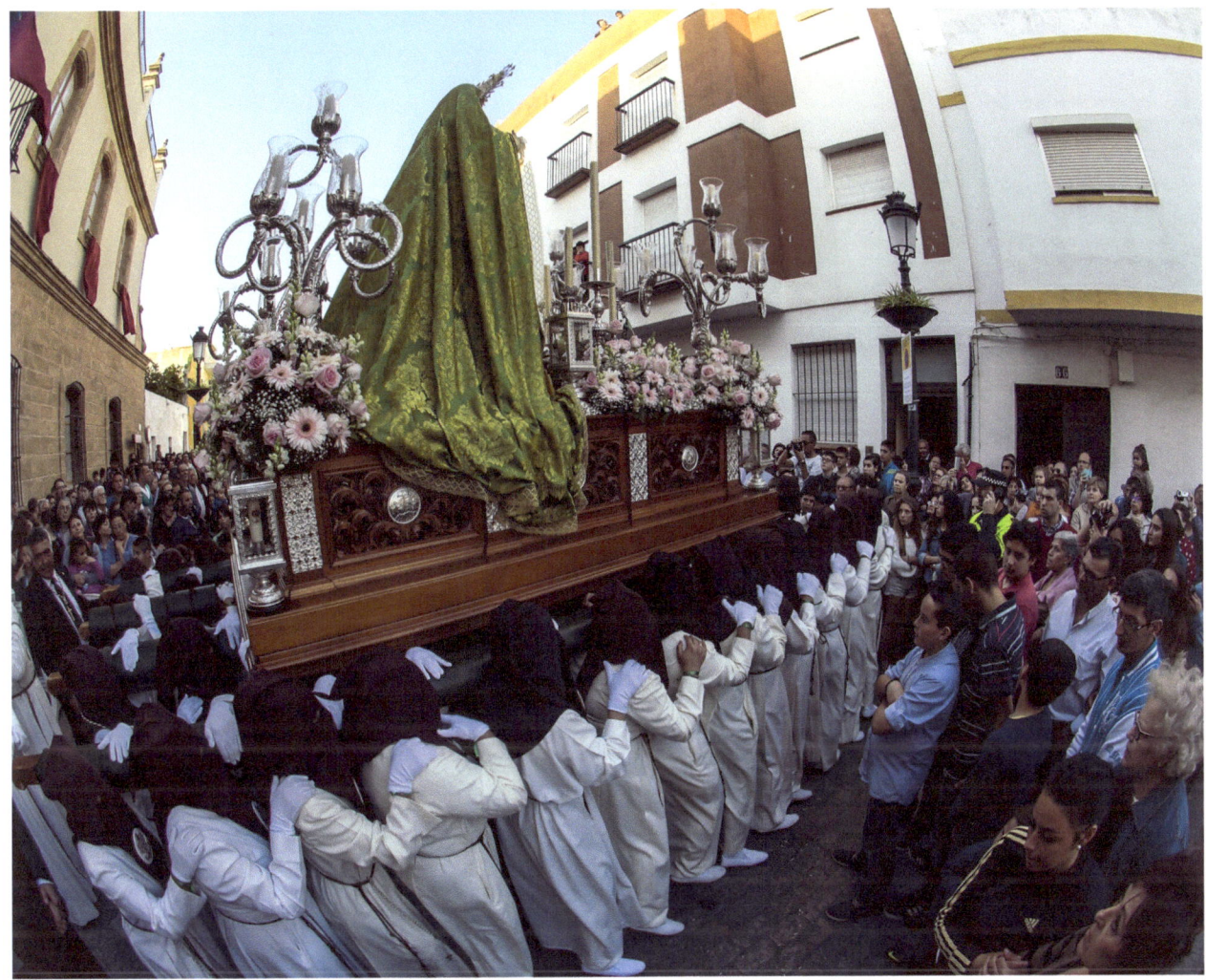

   This incredibly ornate float of the Virgin Mary has the distinction of being carried by all female Costaleras. As they pass through the streets stopping from time to time to rest – the float is set down on built in legs. When they resume, the Costaleros toss the float into the air emphatically stating that they can in fact bear the weight. This act brings much applause from the assembled crowd.

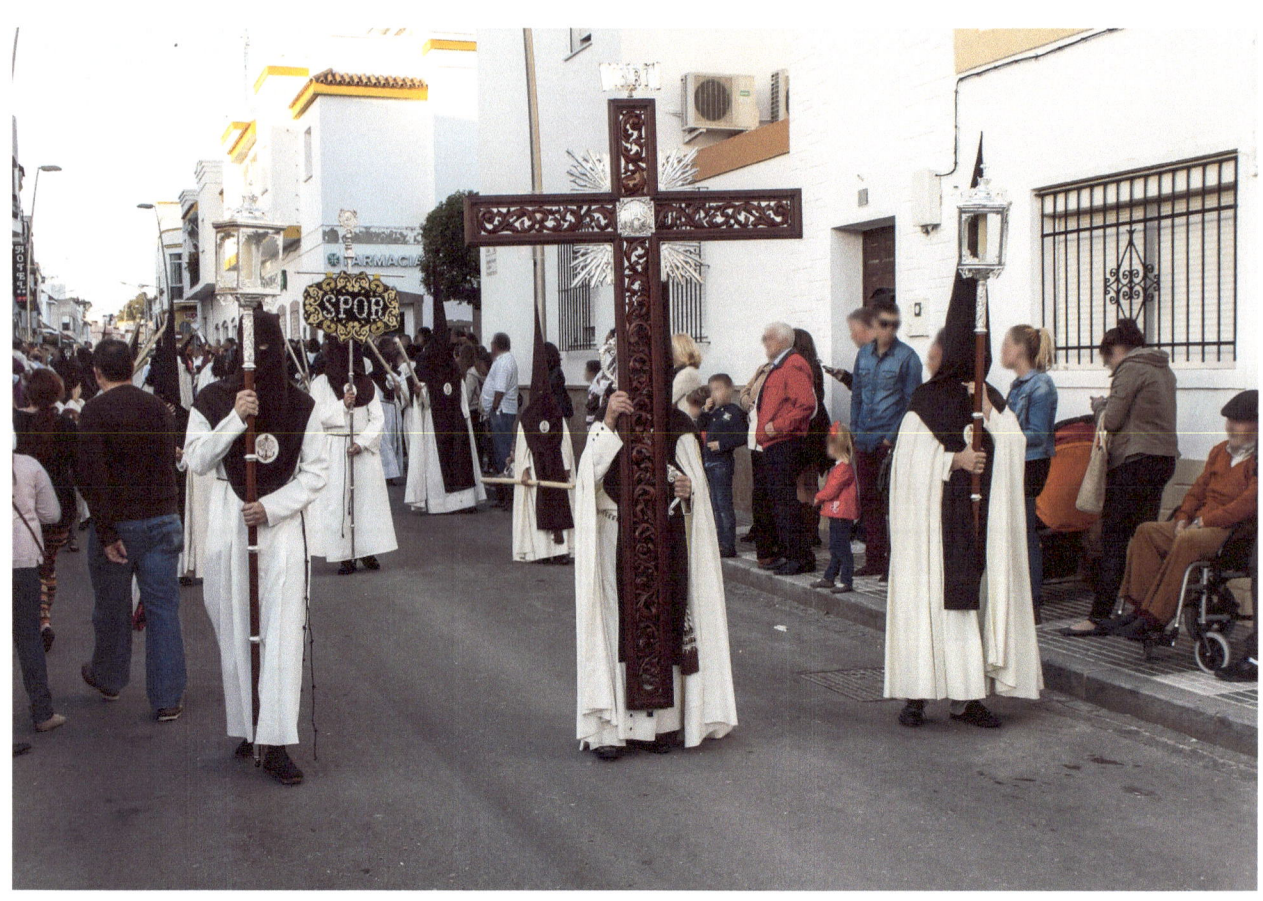

The Guiding Cross (La Cruz de Guia) that leads the Brotherhood through the streets. While they do take breaks when they can set it down, I am sure hours of carrying this cross around is very physically demanding.

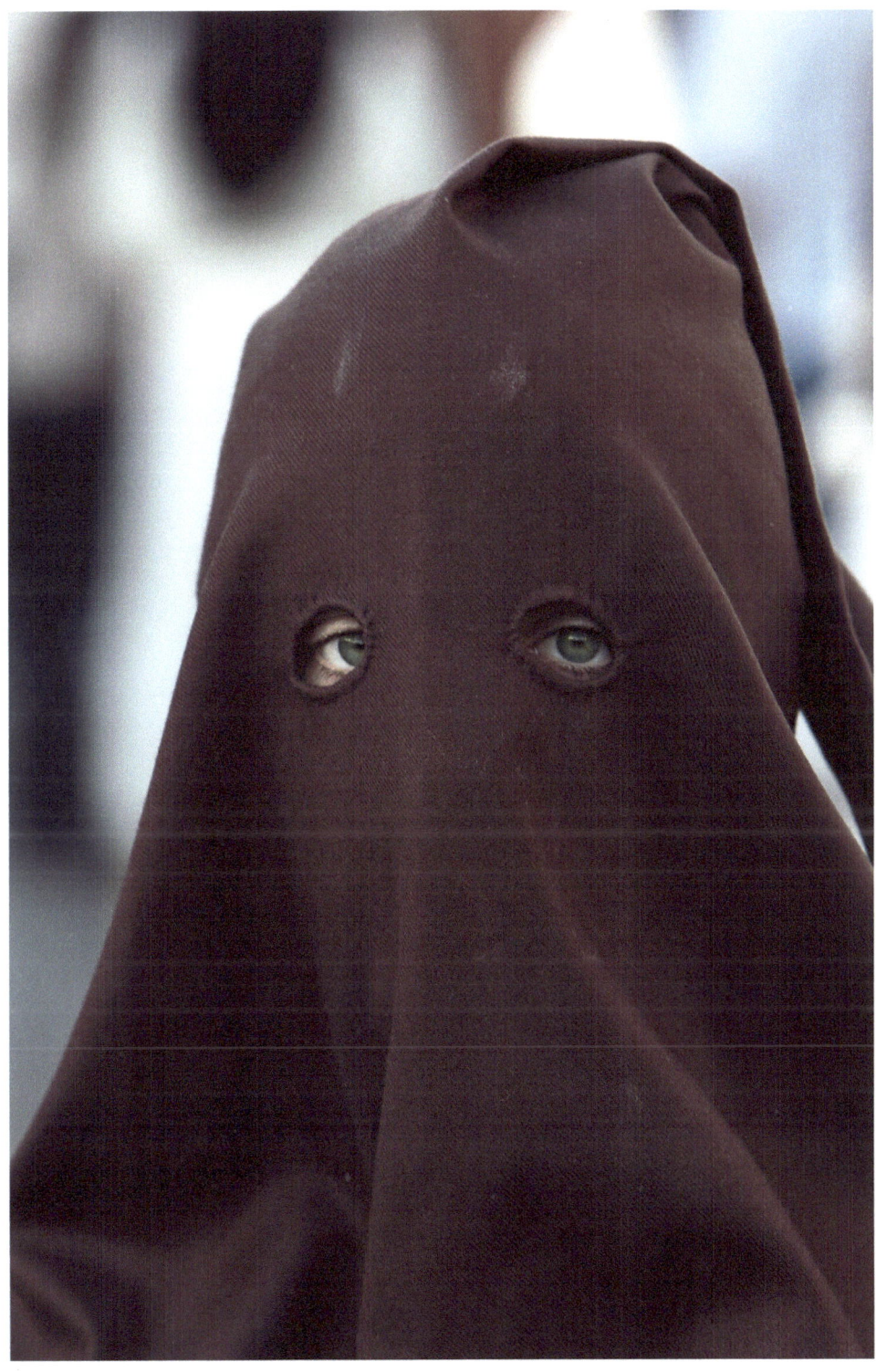

   This girl's eyes just captivated me in a way that I just can't find words to describe. As an artist whose medium is photography I strive for that moment when everything comes together – this is one of those moments. It would not be unusual for me to clean up things on pictures like this one but I found the smears of wax on her Capirote to be too important of a part of the story to take out.

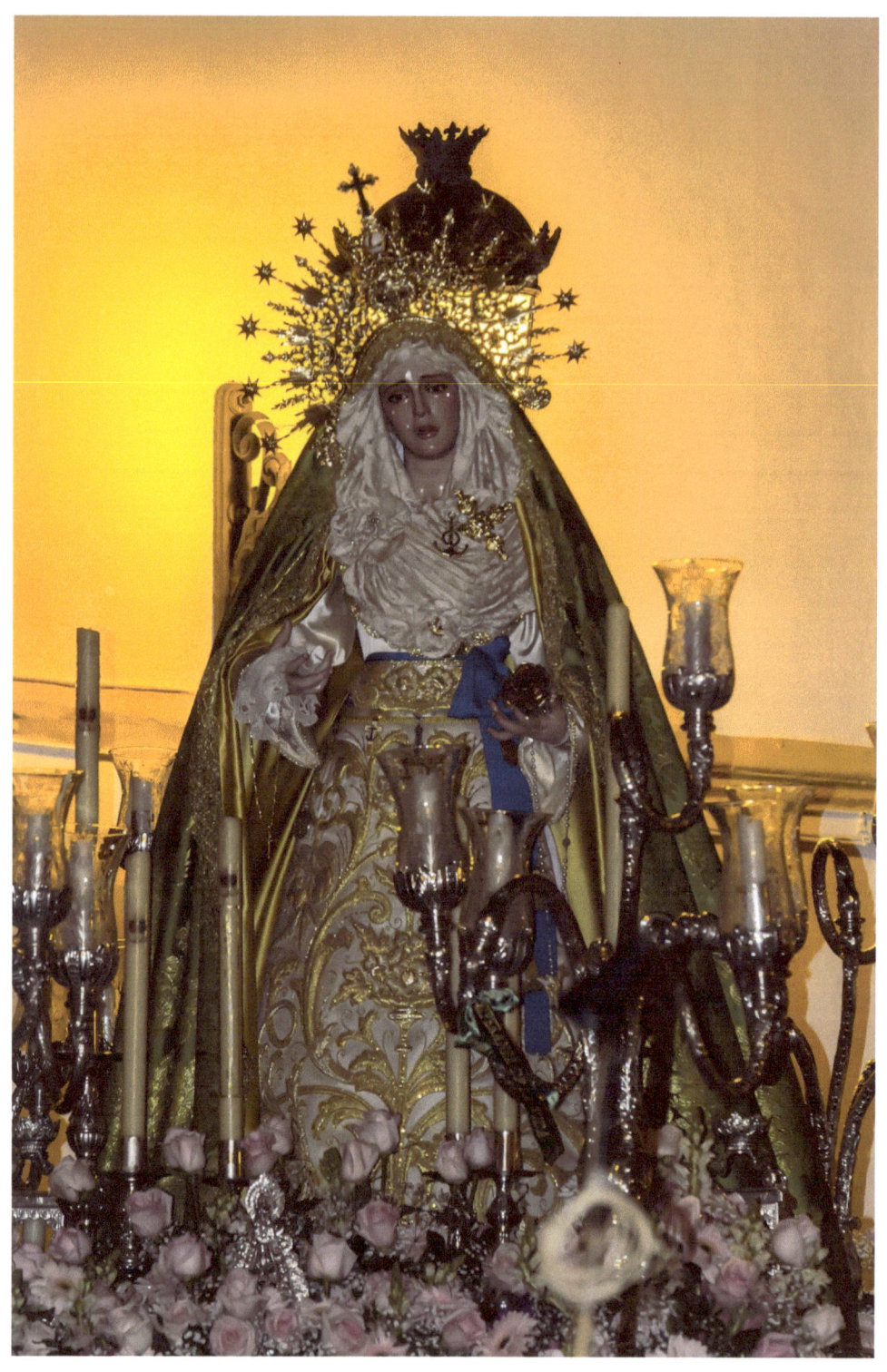

Float of the Virgin Mary with a street light behind her crown. There was a float of the Virgin Mary in all but one procession alluding to the respect toward Mary as the Mother of God that the Catholic Church and Spaniards have.

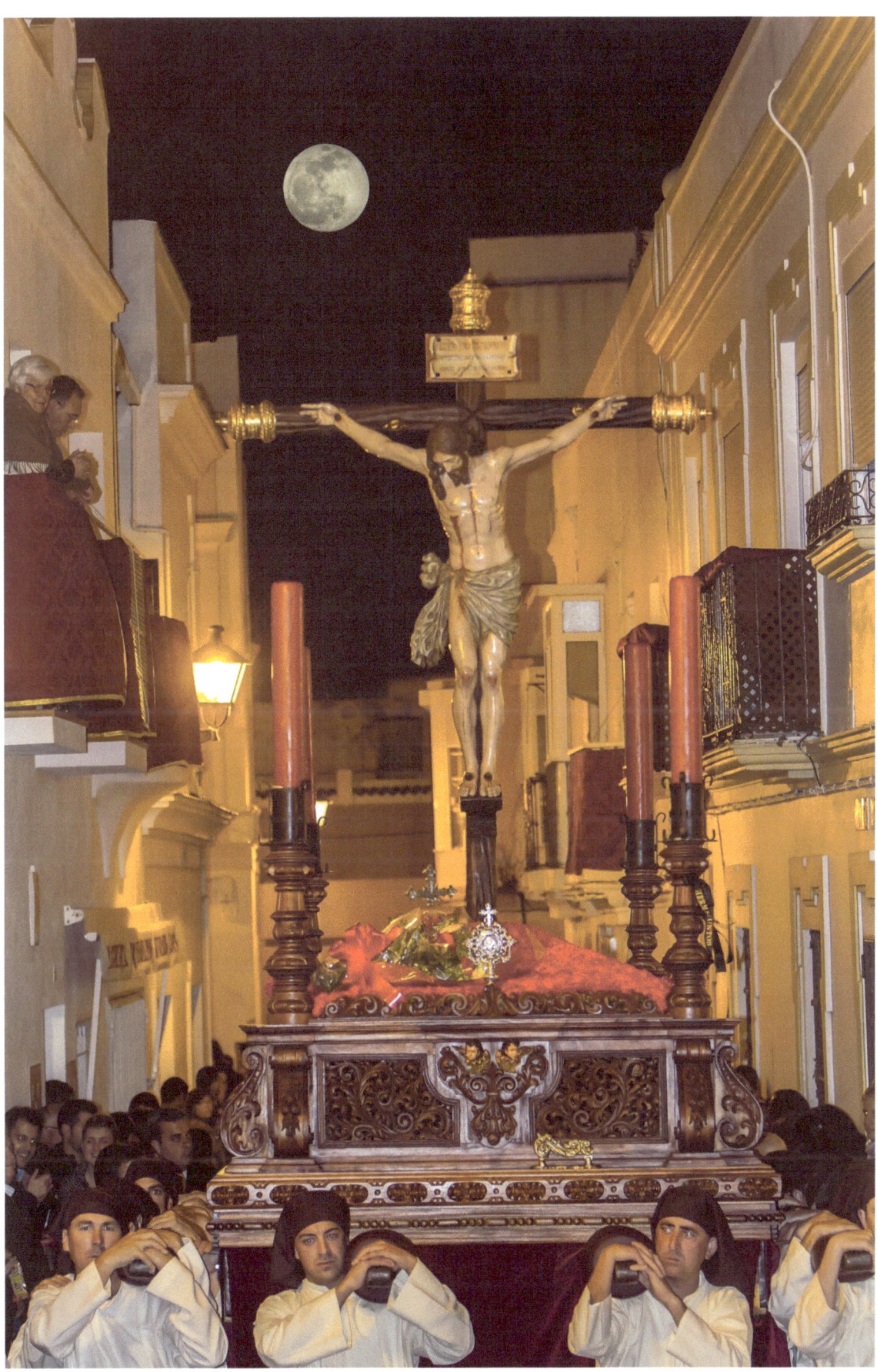

As many who are familiar with my work know I have an affinity toward the Moon and its spiritual symbolism. I was specifically looking for and planning this shot months prior to leaving for Spain. I was overjoyed at being able to be in this spot at this time. With perhaps man's second (the Sun was most likely the first) spiritual symbol and the most iconic spiritual symbol combining elements here touches me deeply as to who we are and the multitudes of generations before me that have gone through this spiritual journey we are on.

Martes Santo (Holy Tuesday), El Puerto de Santa Maria, Spain

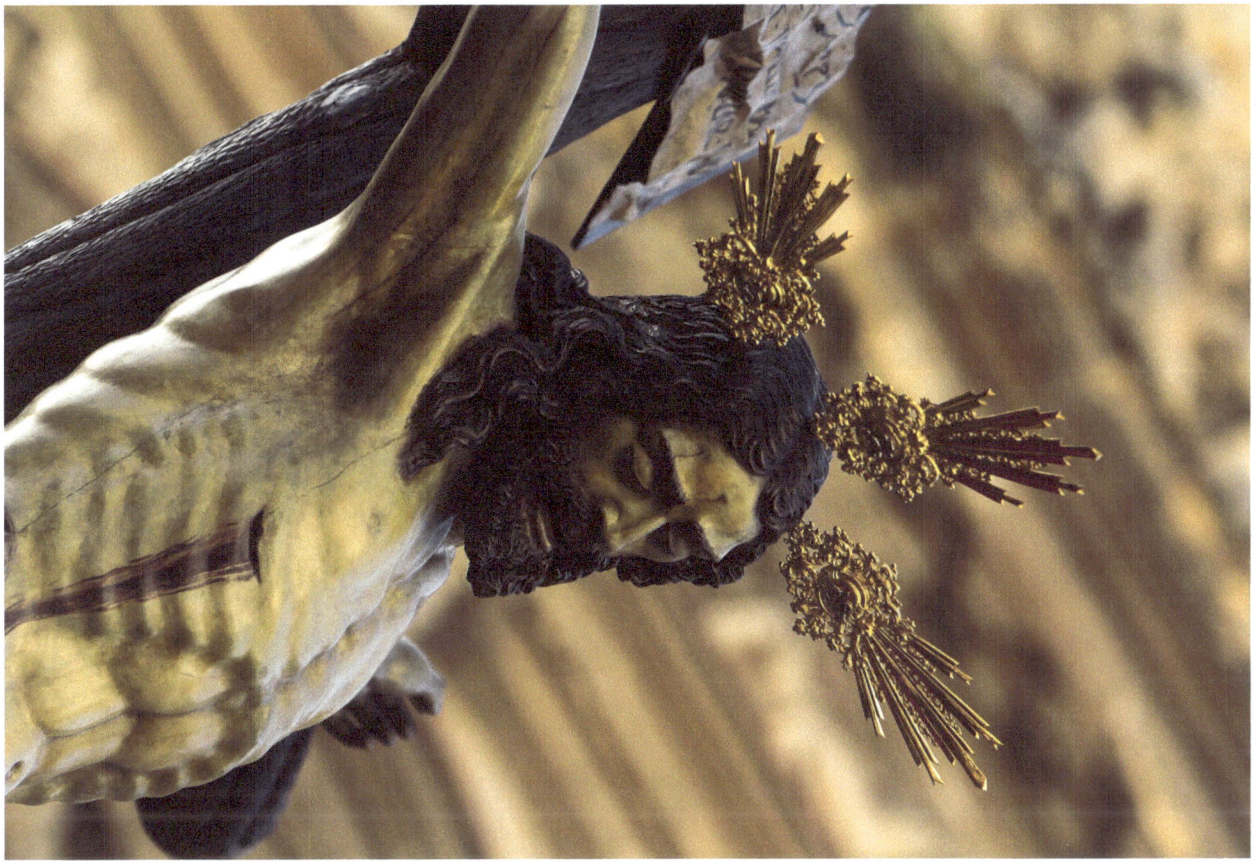

Close up of a crucified Christ with a blurred Priory Church as the background. The sign above Jesus' head here is an exact replica of the original in that it says, "Jesus the Nazarene, King of the Jews" in all three languages (Hebrew, Latin, and Greek).

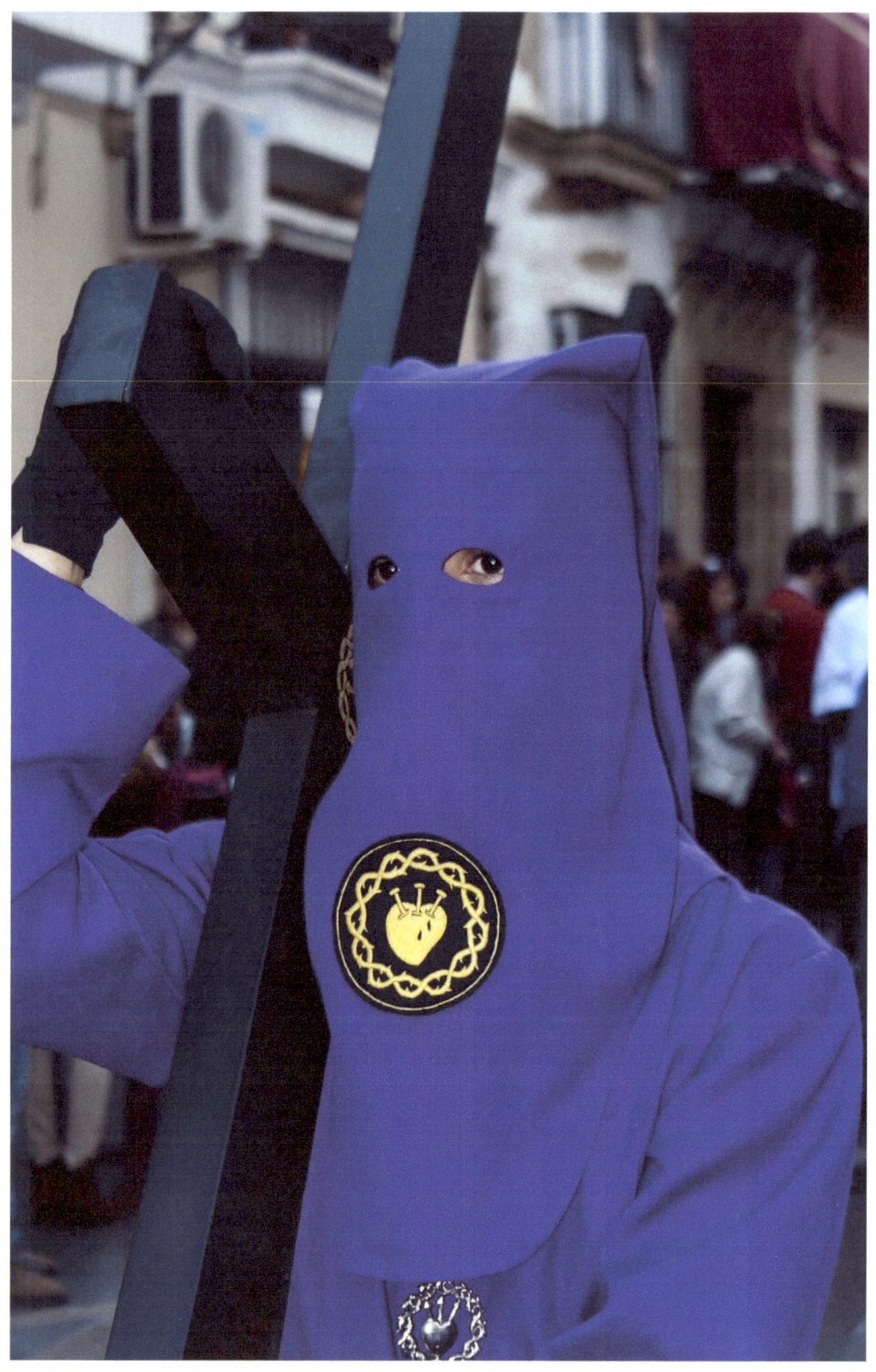

A Penitent carrying a cross. Some Penitents carry two or three crosses at a time as their act of penance. After walking along with the Processions with all my camera gear I have a new found respect for symbolic sacrifice as a means of becoming a more spiritual being. An interesting piece of information I found in my research. The color purple was worn by Roman Emperors and then later by Catholic Bishops and has ever since been associated with royalty and piety.

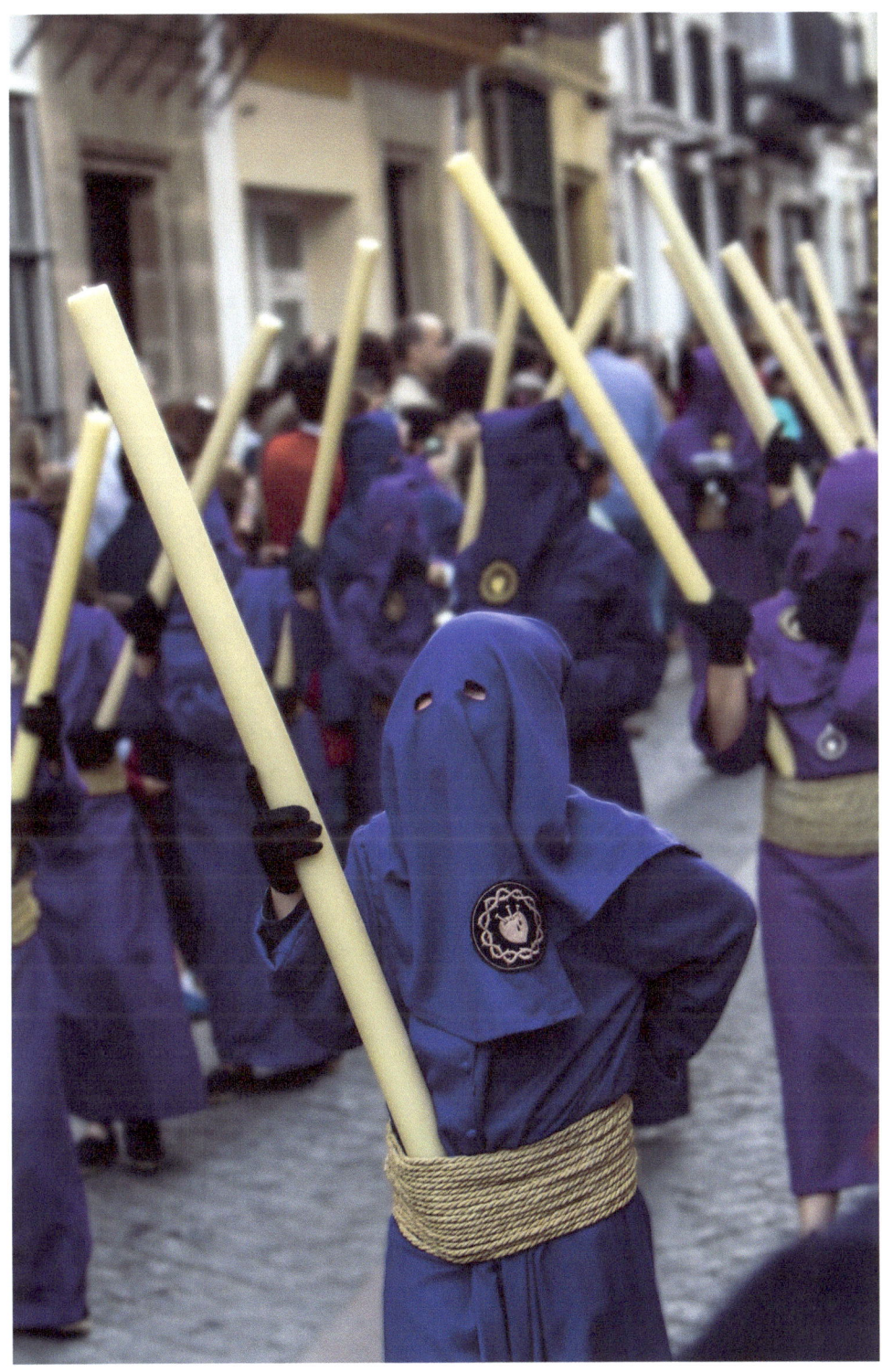

Penitents marching through the streets carrying ceremonial candles. This young Penitent is fighting a sore back from walking too long and at this point still has several hours left to march.

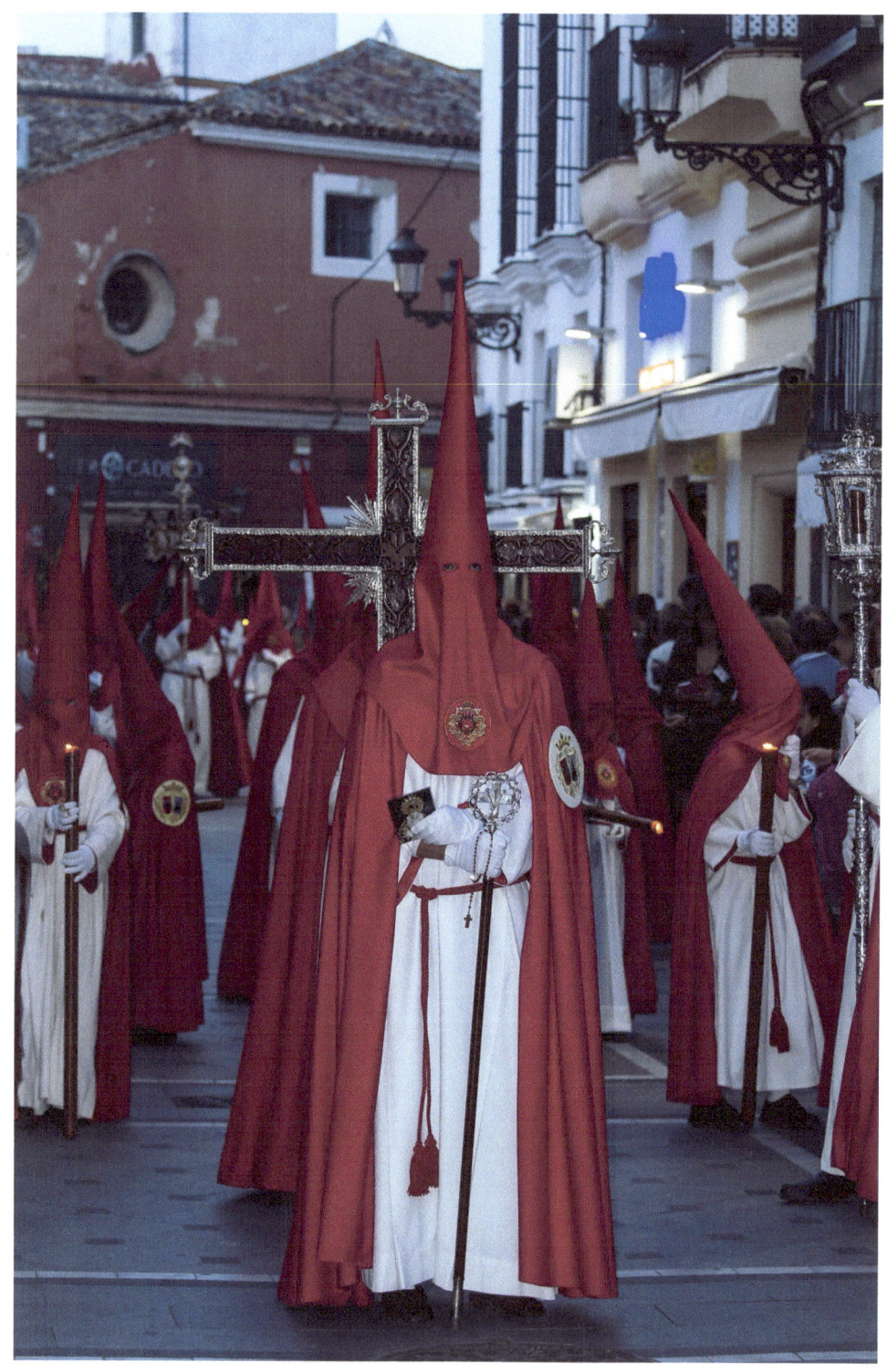

Leading the guiding cross and Brotherhood through the streets. The purpose of wearing a Capirote is to ensure the penance is done anonymously but there were many in the crowd observing who knew exactly who was who. The conversations among observers was quite jovial but more serious when engaging with Penitents.

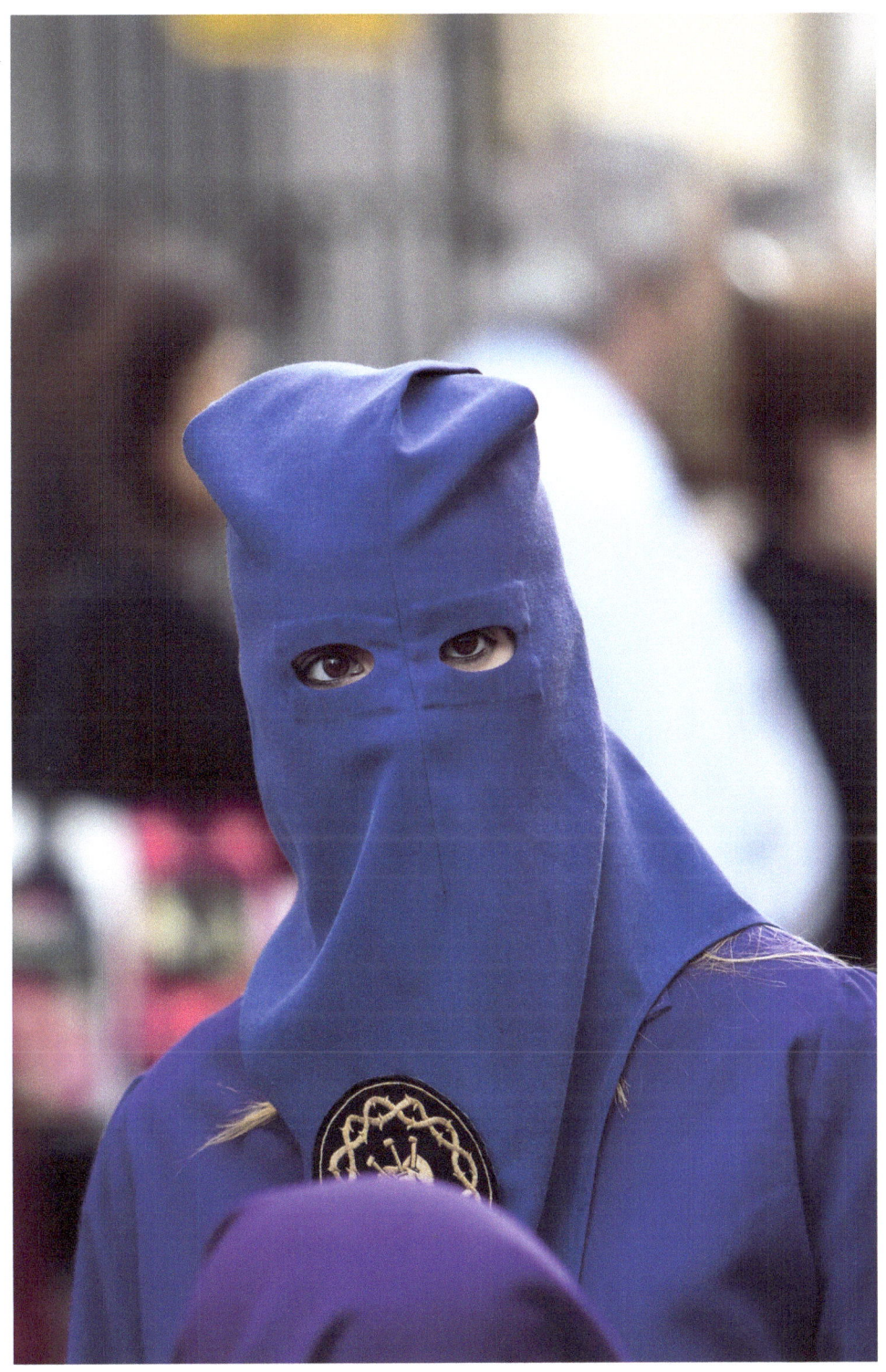

Another display of intense eyes. I have no idea about what her thoughts actually were, but this shot gives me the feeling that she felt I was violating her space simply by taking a picture of her. But the intensity of her gaze is far too compelling to not put her in this book.

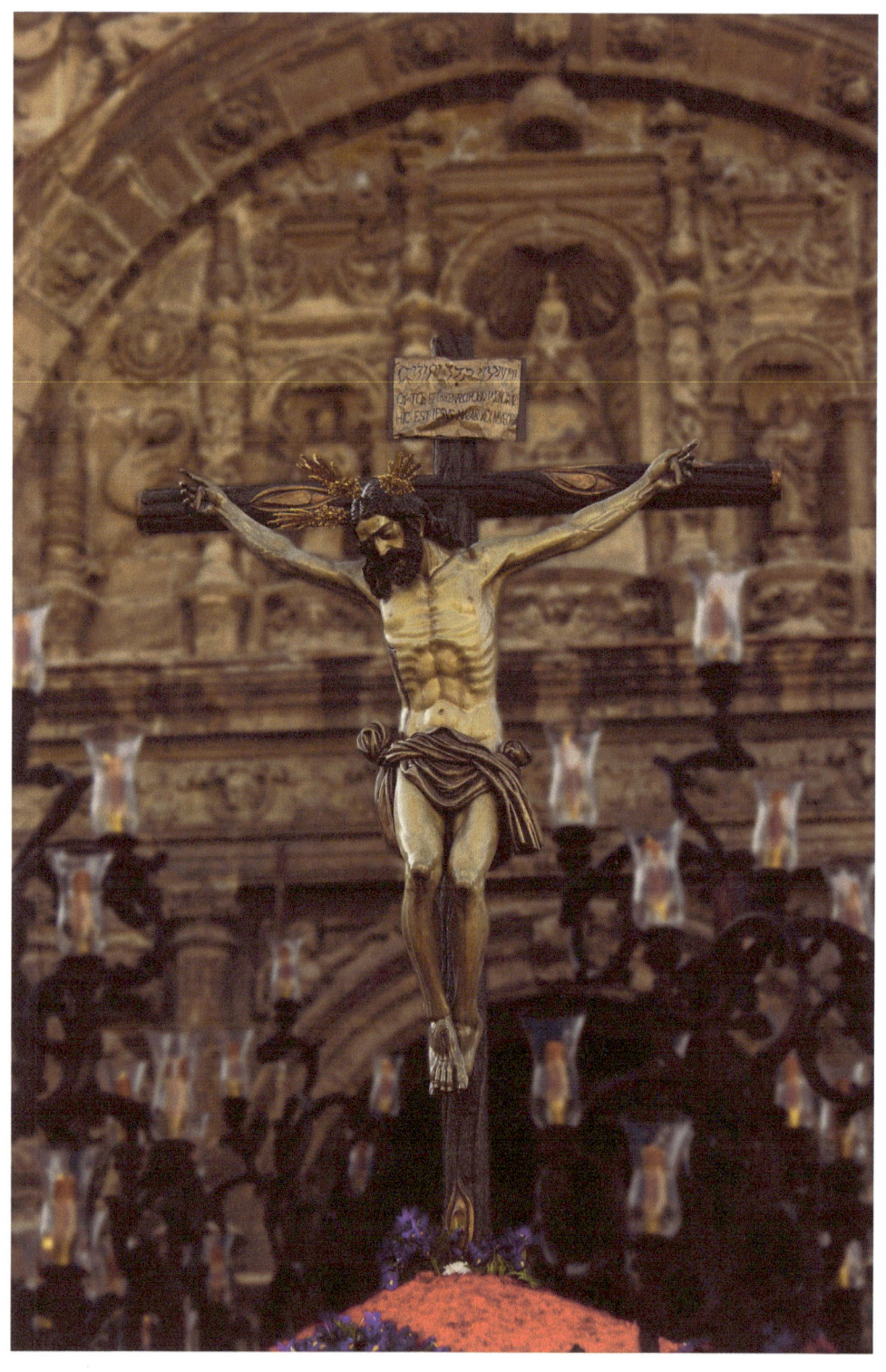

Float of the Crucifixion of Christ in front of Priory Church. This along with many other shots in this book are displayed on the website Fine Art America.

Miércoles Santo (Holy Wednesday), Jerez de la Frontera, Spain

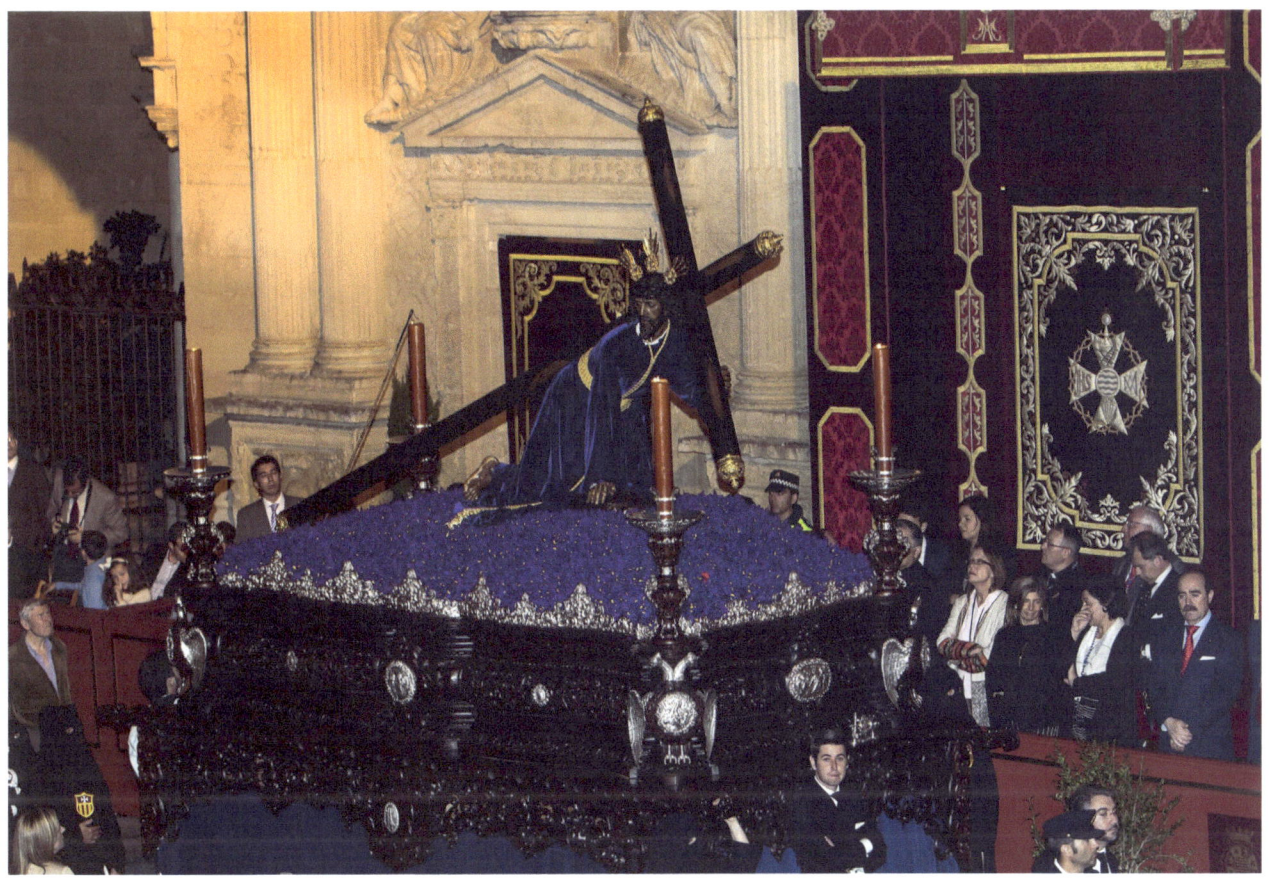

   David Frasier-Luckie graciously allowed absolute strangers, my wife Lynn and I,
into his home and he took time out of his busy day in order to help us understand
and view the Procession in Jerez de la Frontera on Holy Wednesday. We had the
unique perspective of being on a second floor balcony right along the parade route
for much of the Procession allowing us to look down on the crowds, floats, penitents,
and special guests. The above shot of Jesus carrying his cross on a bed of purple
flowers was taken from that balcony as it passed the review stand designated for
dignitaries, officials, and other important people.

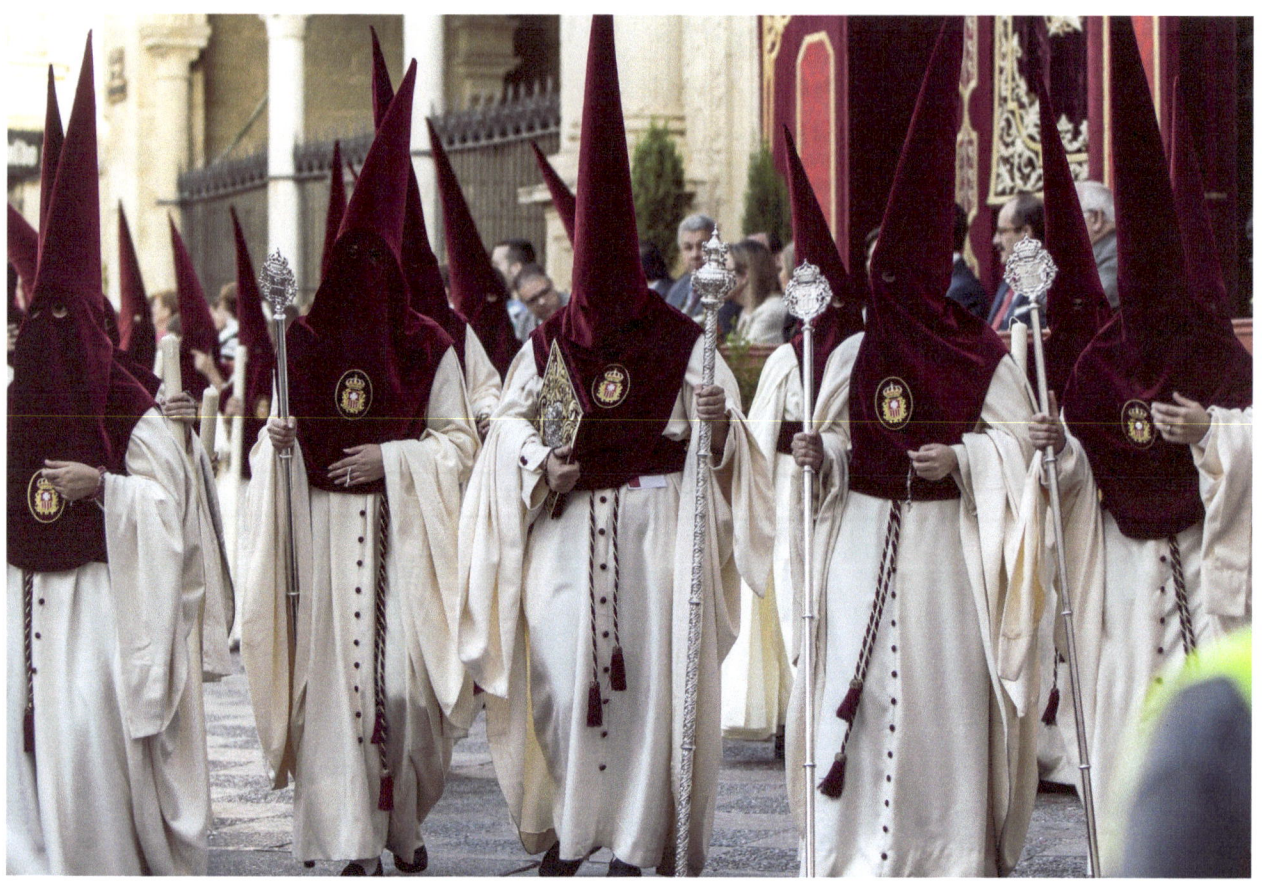

Members of a Brotherhood all in a line. I especially like the expressiveness of each Penitents left hand in this shot. I also like how it shows how big the Capirotes are and how much of a burden having that size of lever on top of your head can be. The book that the center Nazareno is carrying are the rules of their Brotherhood.

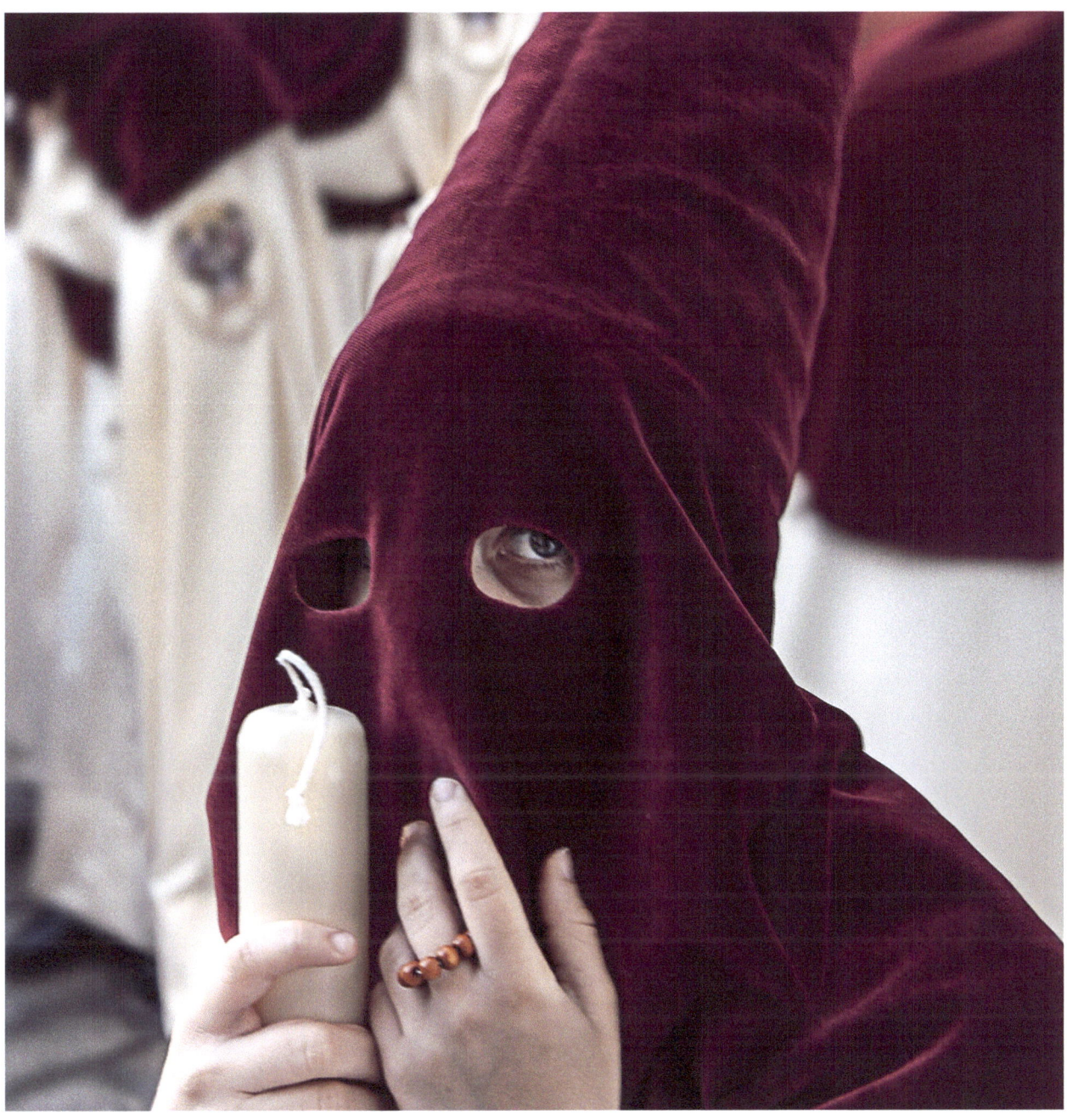

To my eye, this shot captures almost perfectly what I was trying to express the whole time I was there. The beckoning hands and the sense of yearning in the eyes, the proximity of candle and Rosary, and the contrast of skin against the Capirote visually encapsulates a desire for spiritual growth at the most base level.

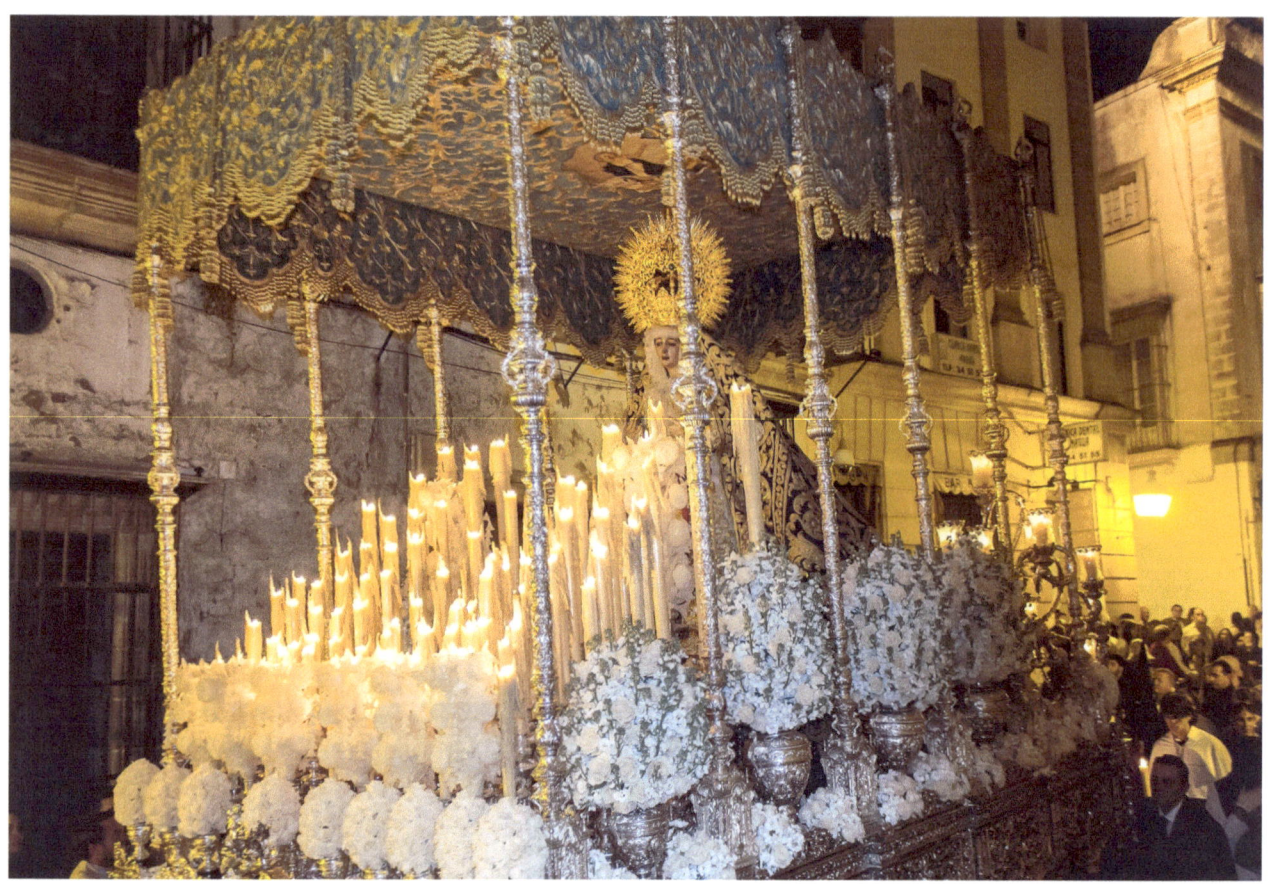

   A float of the Virgin Mary being manipulated through the tight, narrow streets of the ancient city of Jerez de la Frontera. For every float there are two to four people helping the Costaleros maneuver the float safely around tight corners, over curbs, and around crowds. With most floats, the Costaleros have very limited vision if any at all.

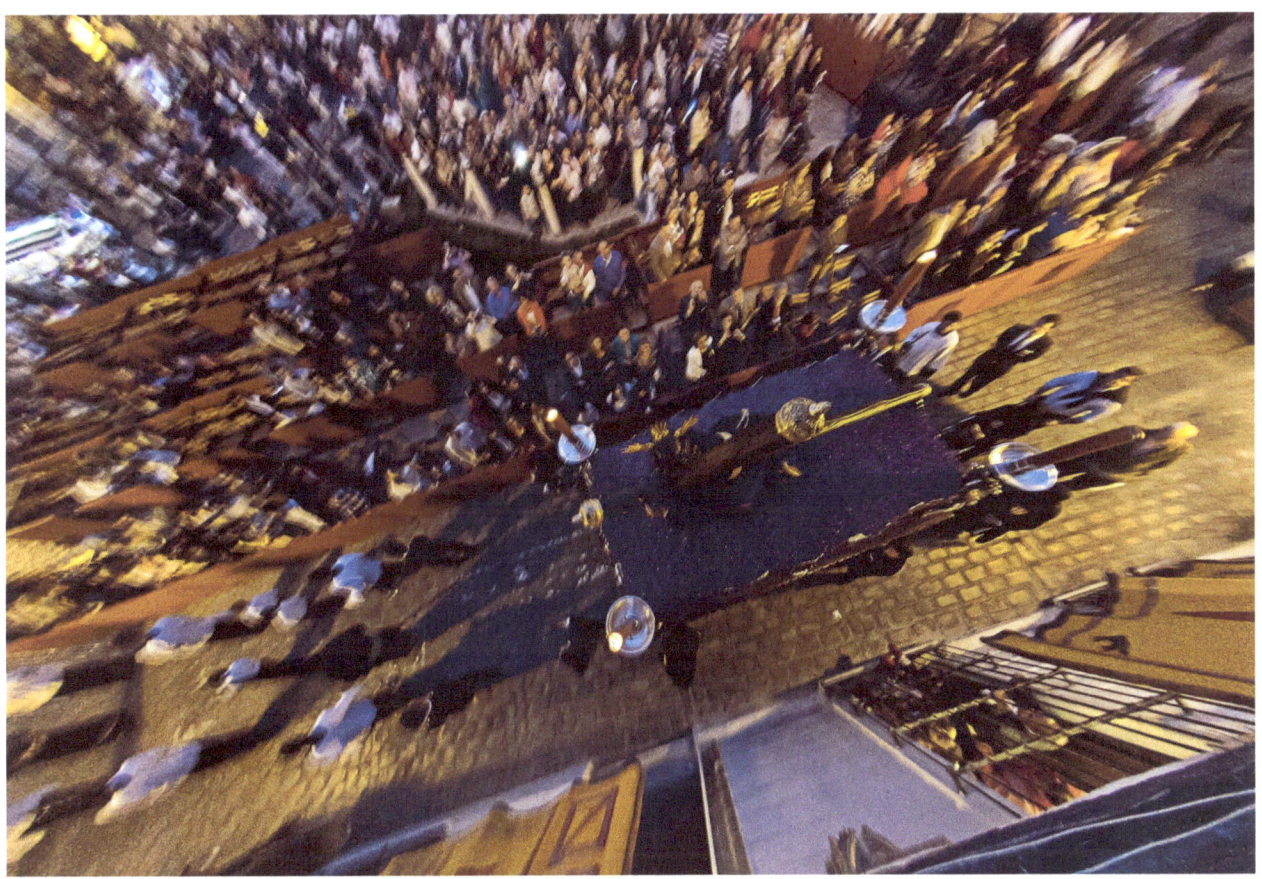

This is a shot with a fisheye lens looking directly down on the float of Christ carrying his cross. What I like about the symbolism of this abstraction is the clearness at
the center (the closest point of the cross and Jesus' head) while the further you get
from the center the more distorted everything becomes.

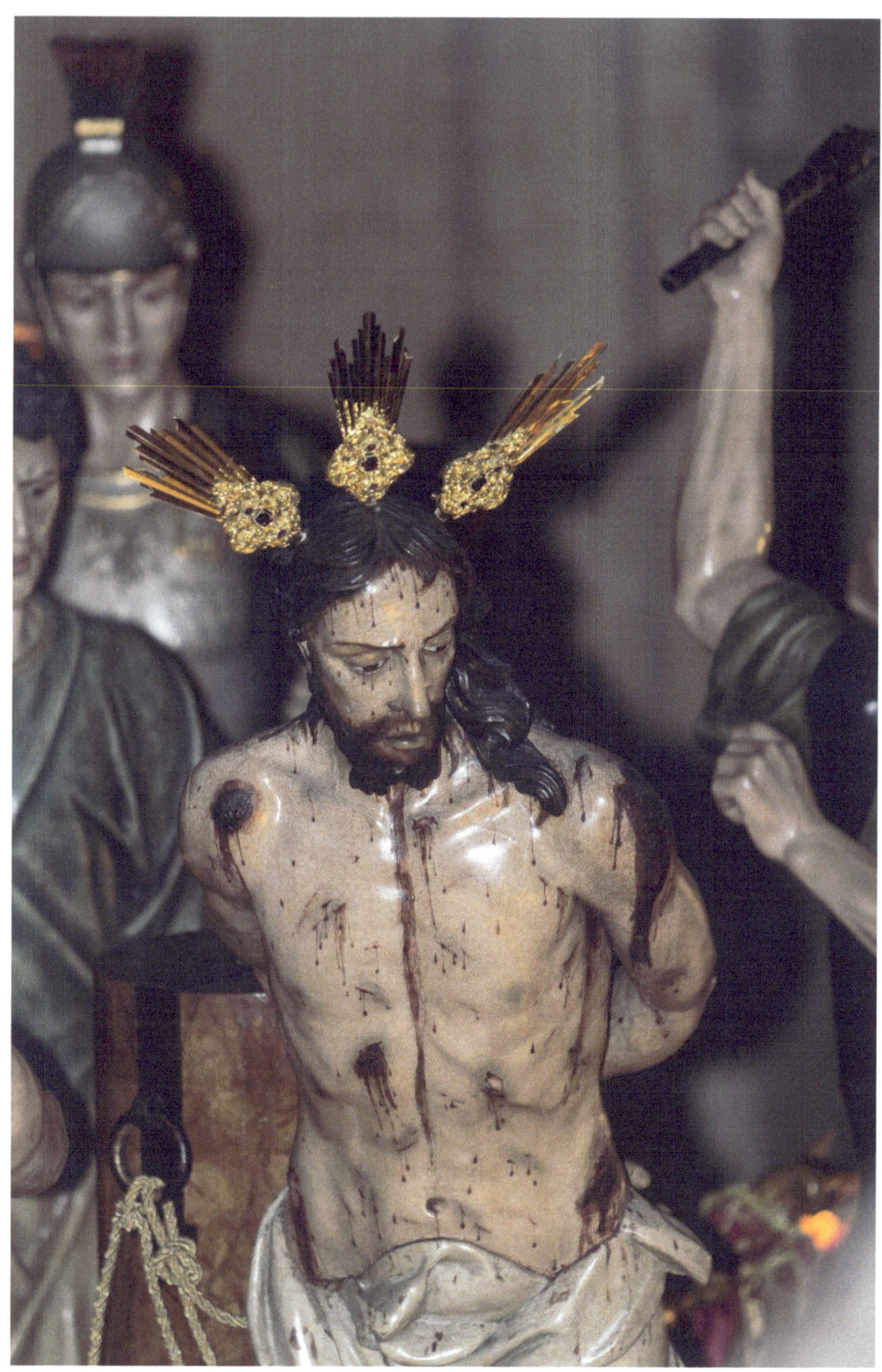

Close up of a float showing the Flagellation of Christ. While I took many shots of this float, I thought this shot showed the essence of the scene best. I particularly like seeing only the arm of the flogger and the other two people play insignificant roles in the scene while a beaten and stigmatized Christ dominates the central vertical.

Jueves Santo (Holy Thursday), Rota, Spain

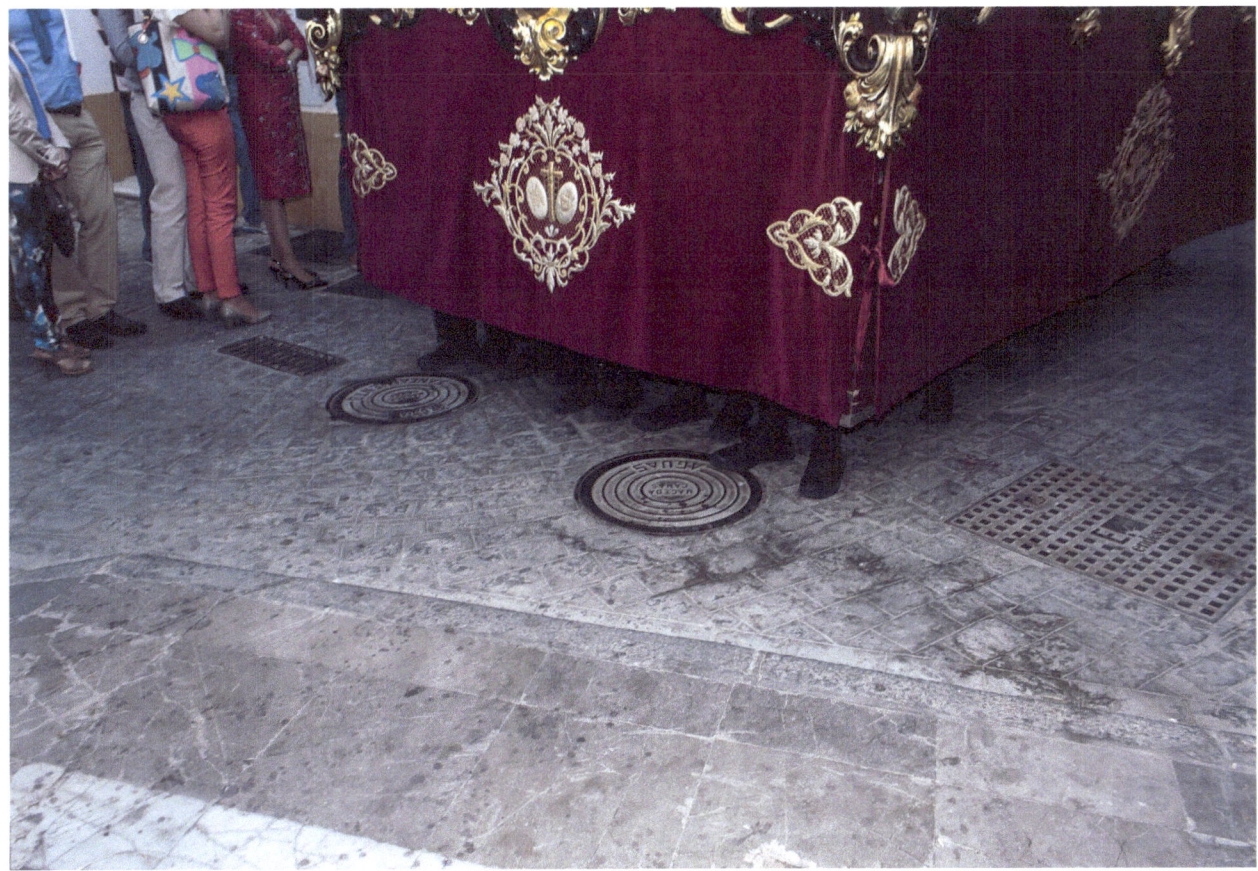

   My intent with this picture is to give a feel for what it is like to be a Costalero. If you count carefully you can see that there are five people per row and there are six rows for a total of 30 people in a very confined space. Depending on the float, maybe two or four Costaleros can see out of a small hole in front of them but even then vision is extremely limited. As they move through the streets, they rhythmically sway the float from side to side – a movement they have clearly practiced – which helps to animate the scene from the spectators point of view. They do rest periodically and after each rest they actually throw the float into the air. A guilty conscience seems to be a much heavier burden than the weight of the float.

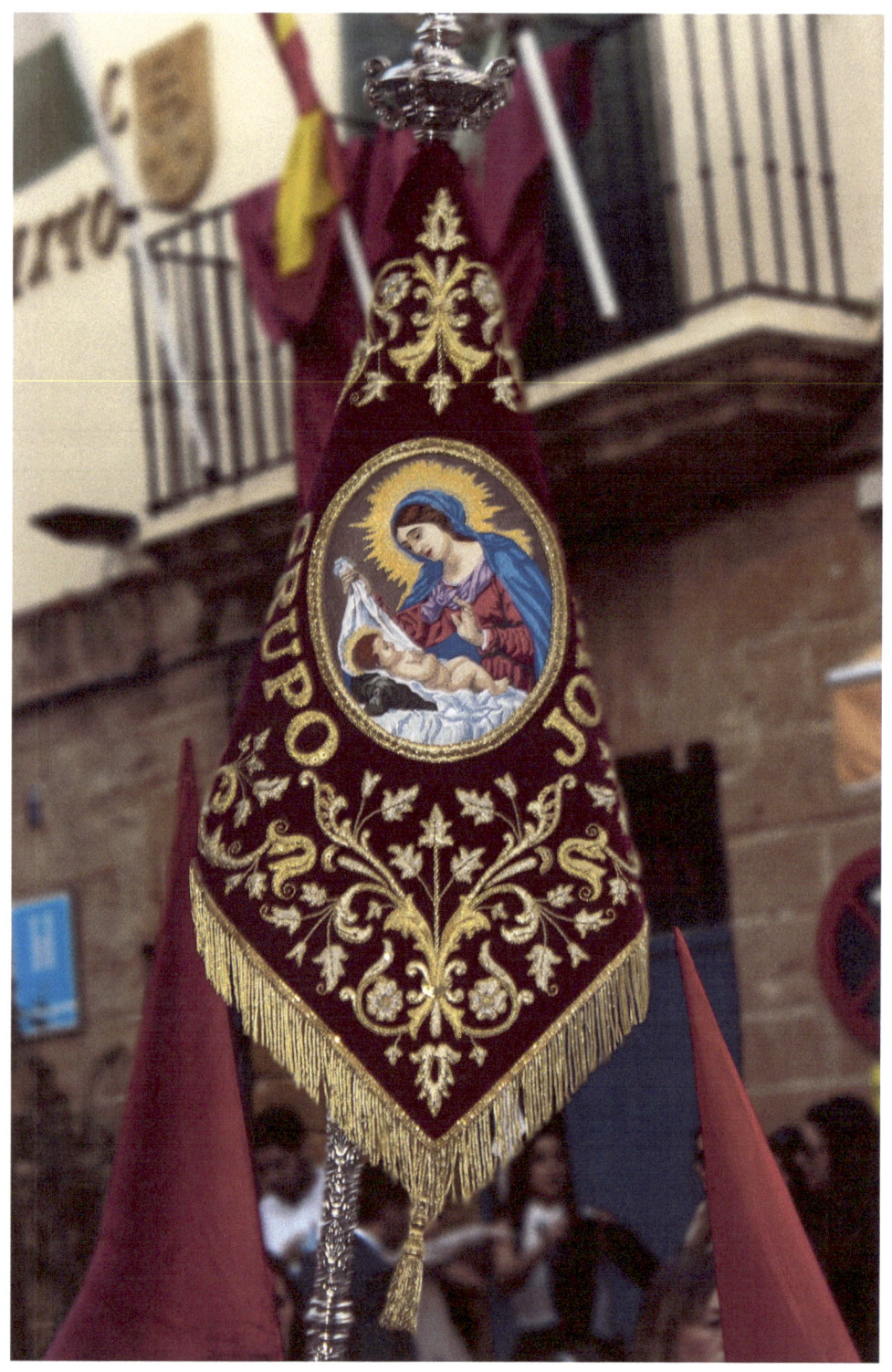

The guiding flag for the "Grupo Joven" (the Young Group). I was genuinely sur-
prised by the number of young participants there were in all the Processions. Many
Fathers and Grandfathers actually carried their babies in the procession.

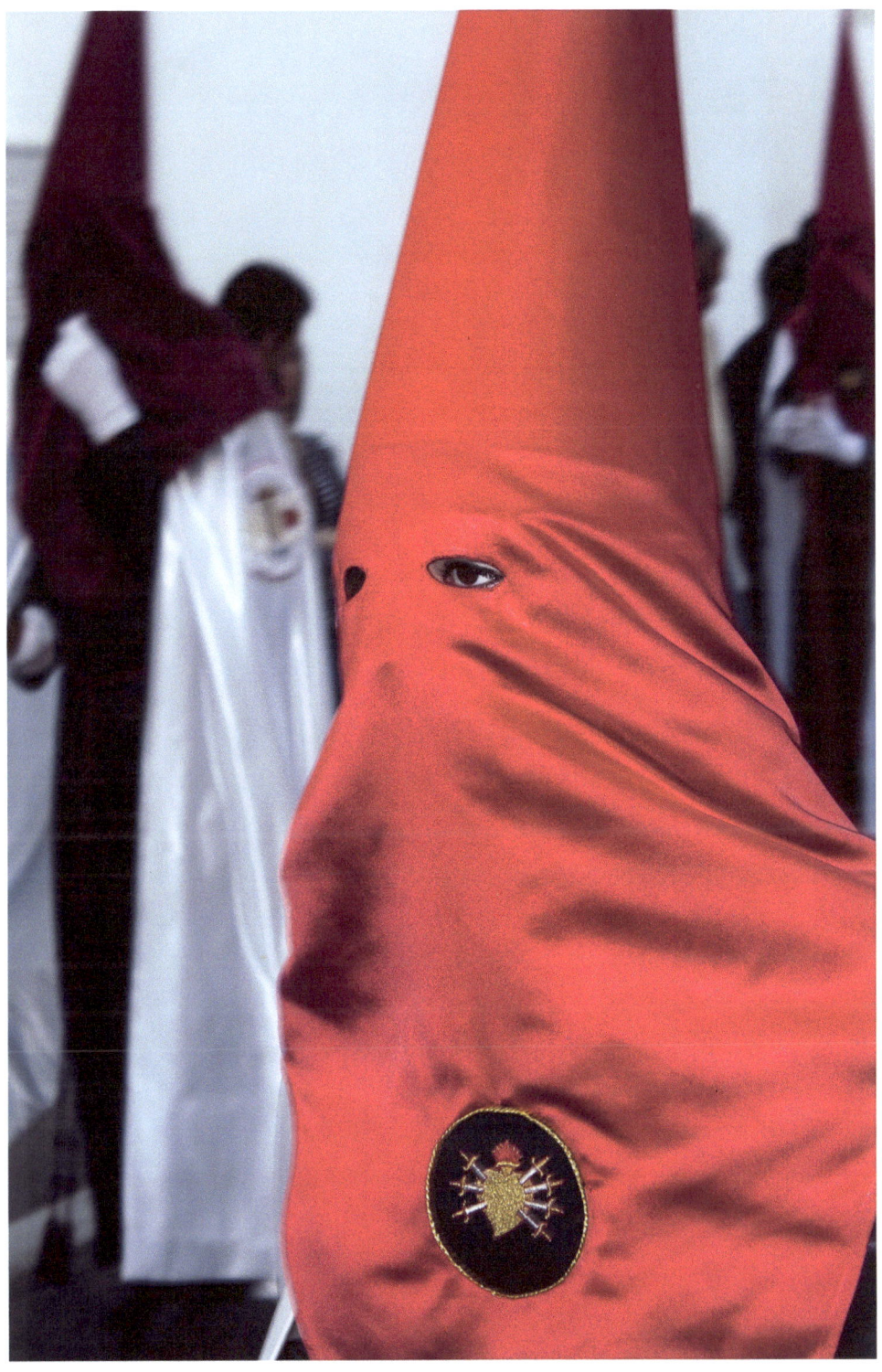

I found the movement from right to left in this shot to be a great symbol of the struggle that it takes to become spiritually enlighten. Even the folds in the Capirote and the determined eye allude to the battle that spiritual fitness requires.

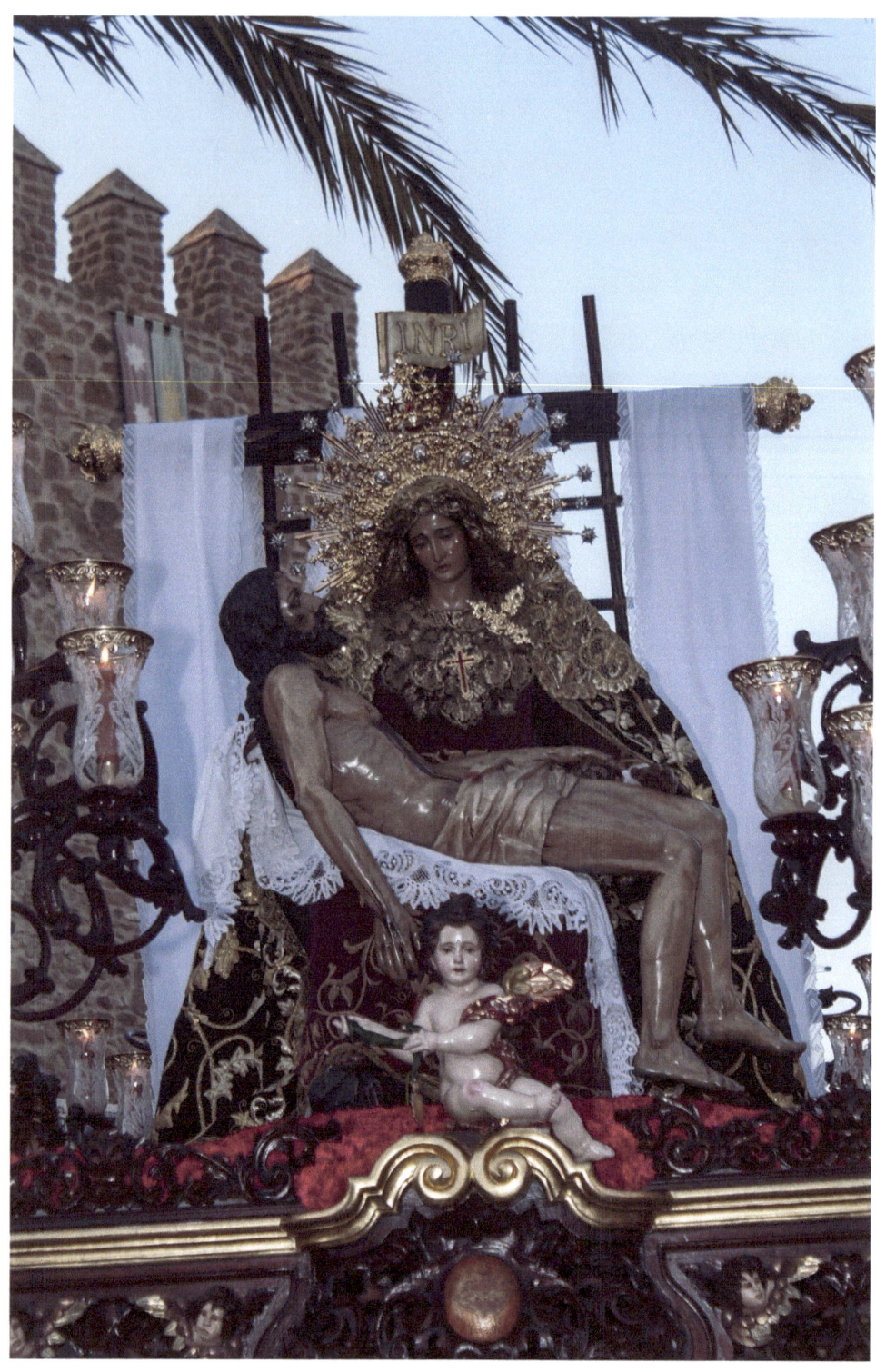

This float was my personal favorite. The detail and craftsmanship at every level and in every element was extraordinary. But more than that, it captures the essence of the transition from Earth to Heaven and the concept that the path to glory is through the Cross.

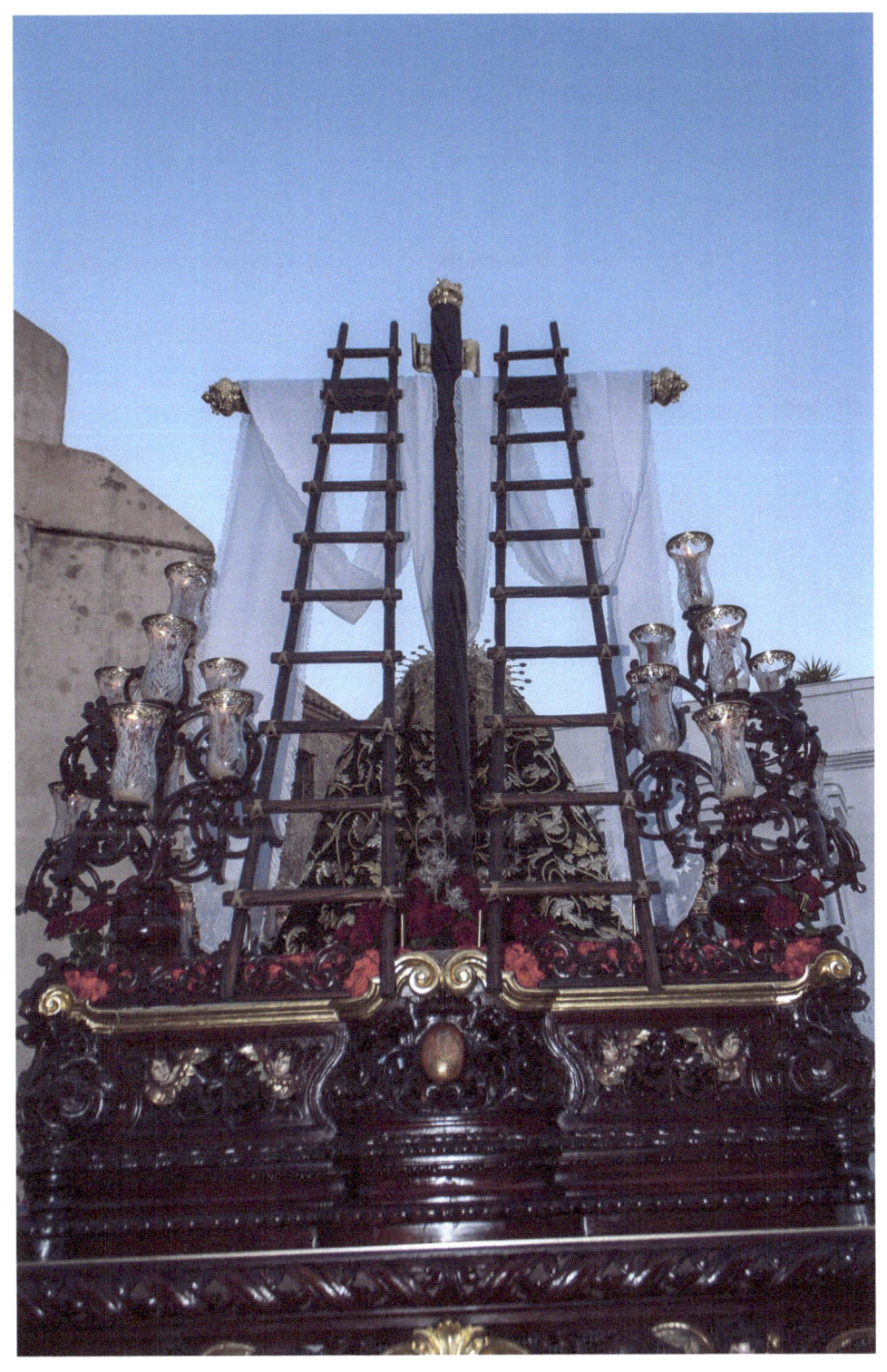

View from the back. While the ladders have the functional purpose of taking Christ down from the Cross, they symbolically also display the ascension to Heaven.

Viernes Santo (Good Friday), Rota, Spain

On Good Friday there were actually three Processions; the 1st one from 2:00AM until 12:00PM, the 2nd from 7:15PM until 12:30AM, and the 3rd from 8:00PM until 1:30AM. I have divided them into two sections here; morning for the one going from 2:00AM until noon and the other two into an evening section.

Morning

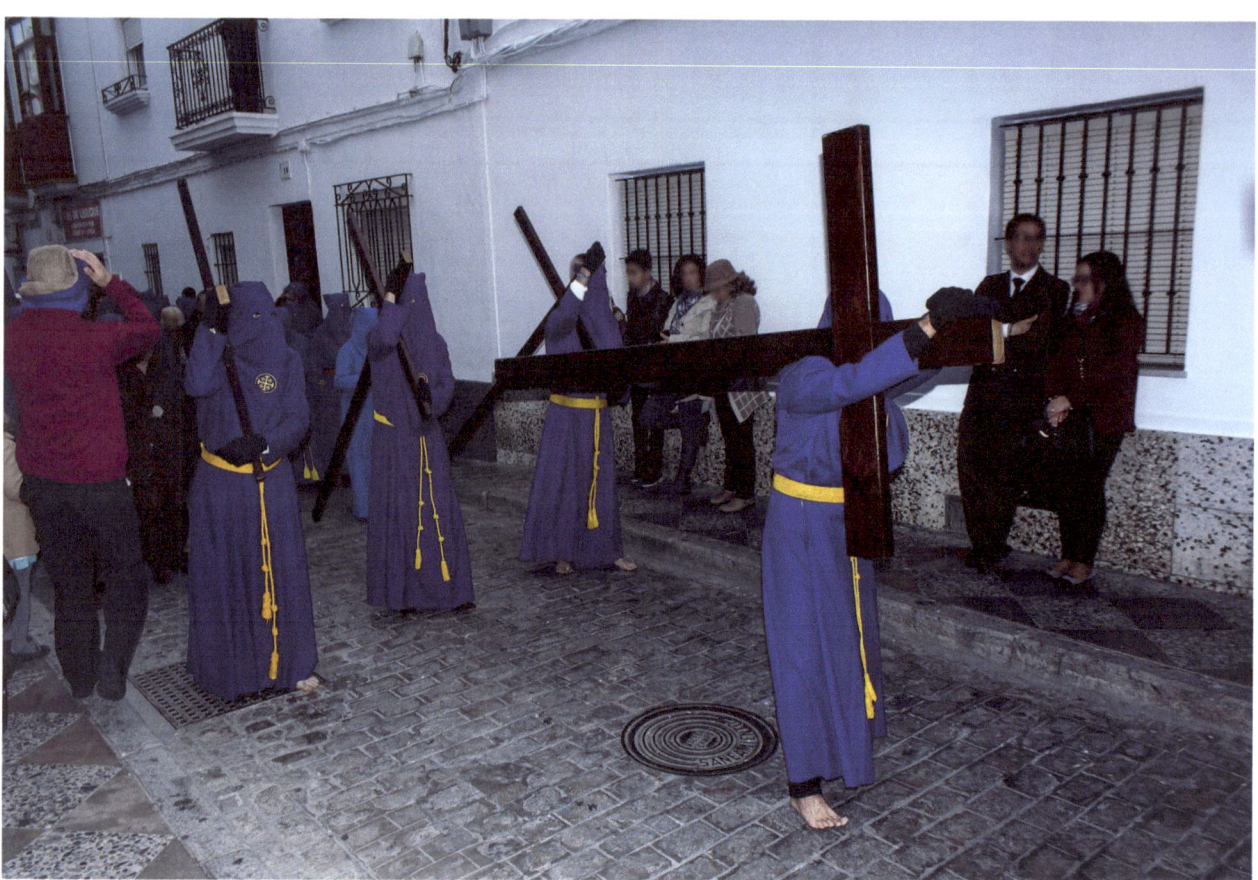

Penitents carrying Crosses. This was taken at about 6:00AM so they are not even half way through their march. I am sure that wooden crosses become quite the burden on the shoulder. Also note that three out of the four Penitents carrying crosses are clearly barefoot. While it wasn't terribly cold, I'm certain this was quite uncomfortable for that much time on cobblestone streets.

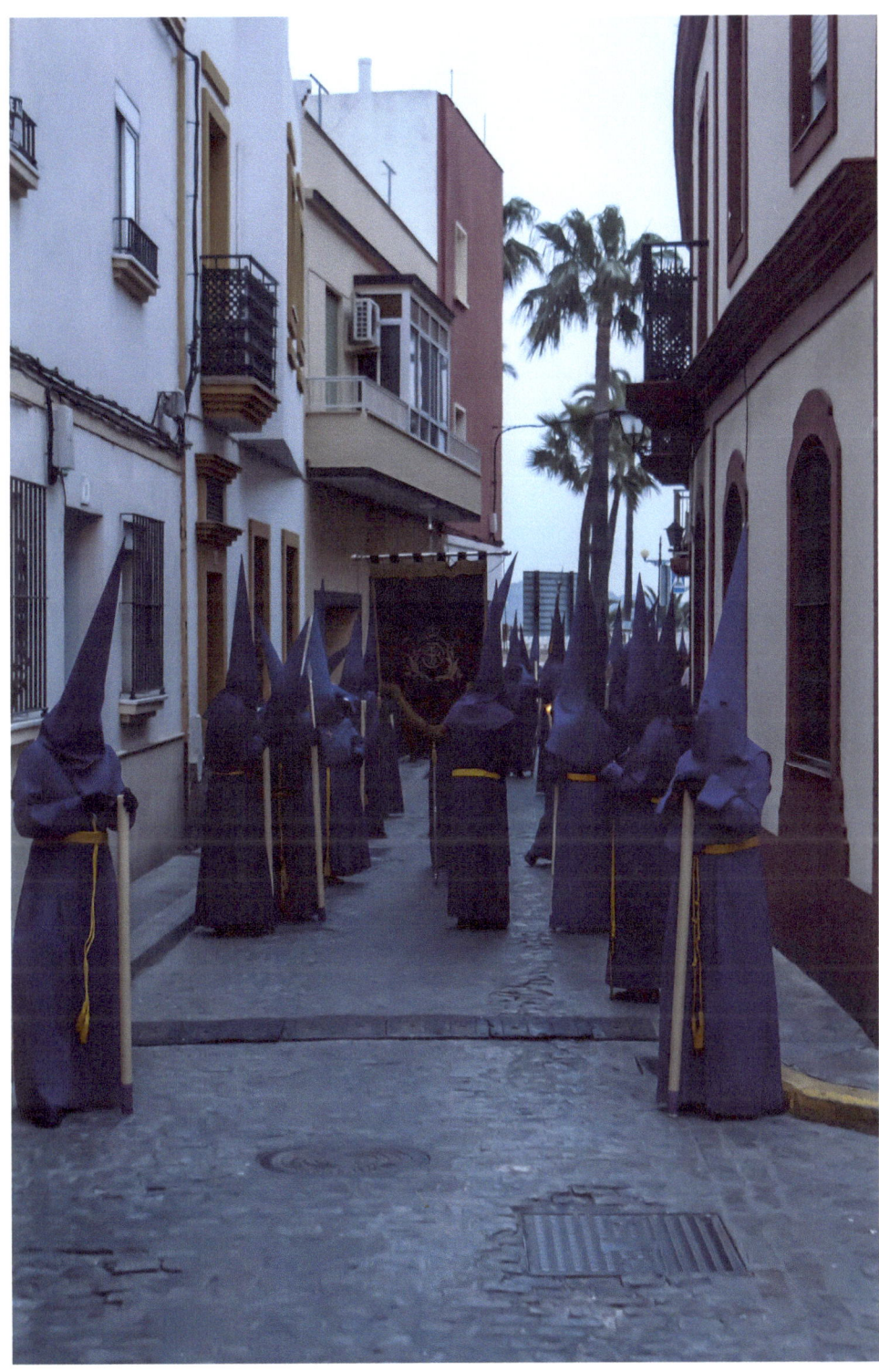

   A spirited stream of penitents on a gloomy sunrise with palm trees in the background. Most of their candles were not lit due to high winds at this time of day but
with nightly Processions burning hundreds and hundreds of candles, quite a bit of
wax gets deposited on the streets. Just driving over the wax causes the tires to
squeal for weeks after the ceremonies.

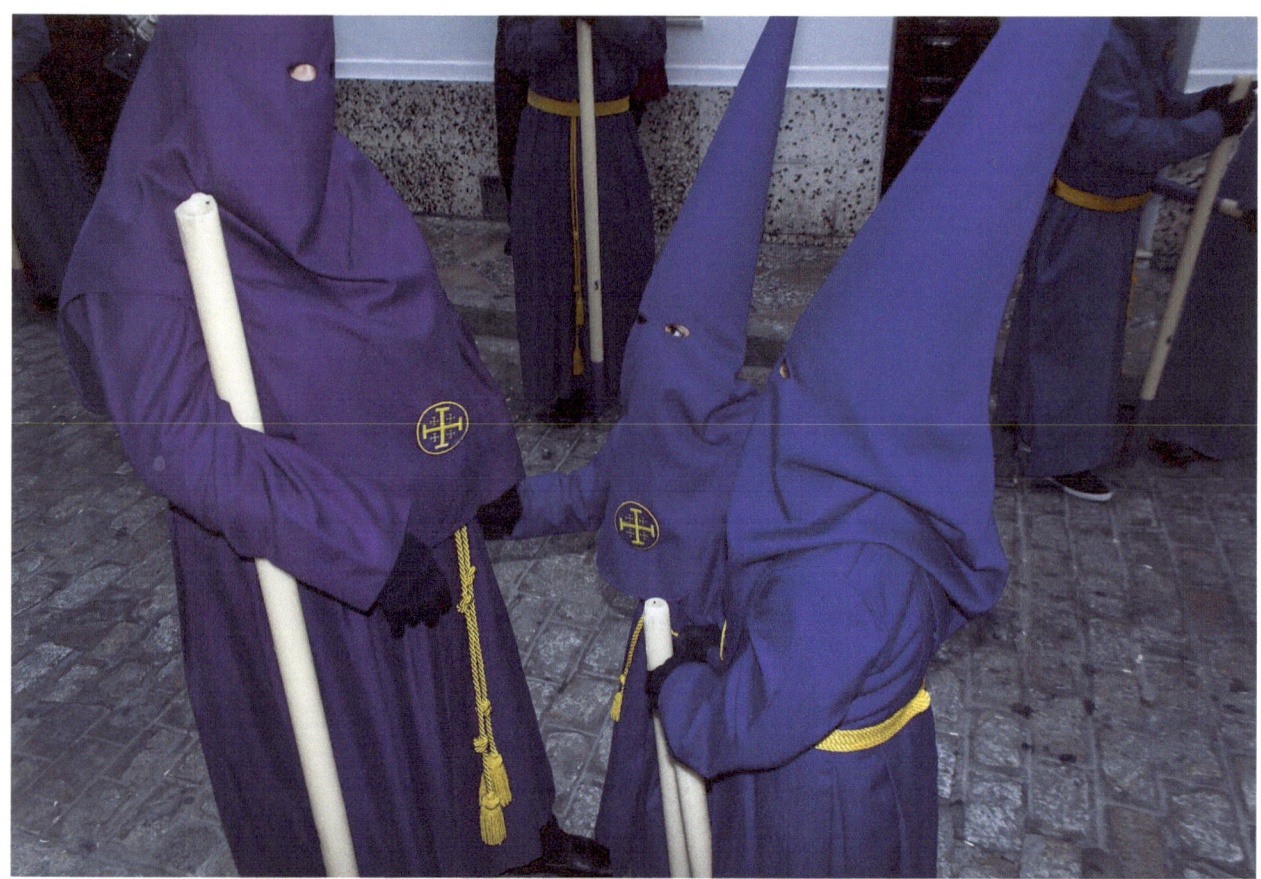

Here a Mother comforts her two children while the Procession is stopped. I would say the younger of the two was eight to ten years old which amazes me that children that young are participating in a ten hour long procession. I've got to hand it to them as they both seemed interested and engaged in the ceremony. Another thing they do to engage the children is to have them collect wax from Nazarenos' candles to see who can make the biggest ball of wax.

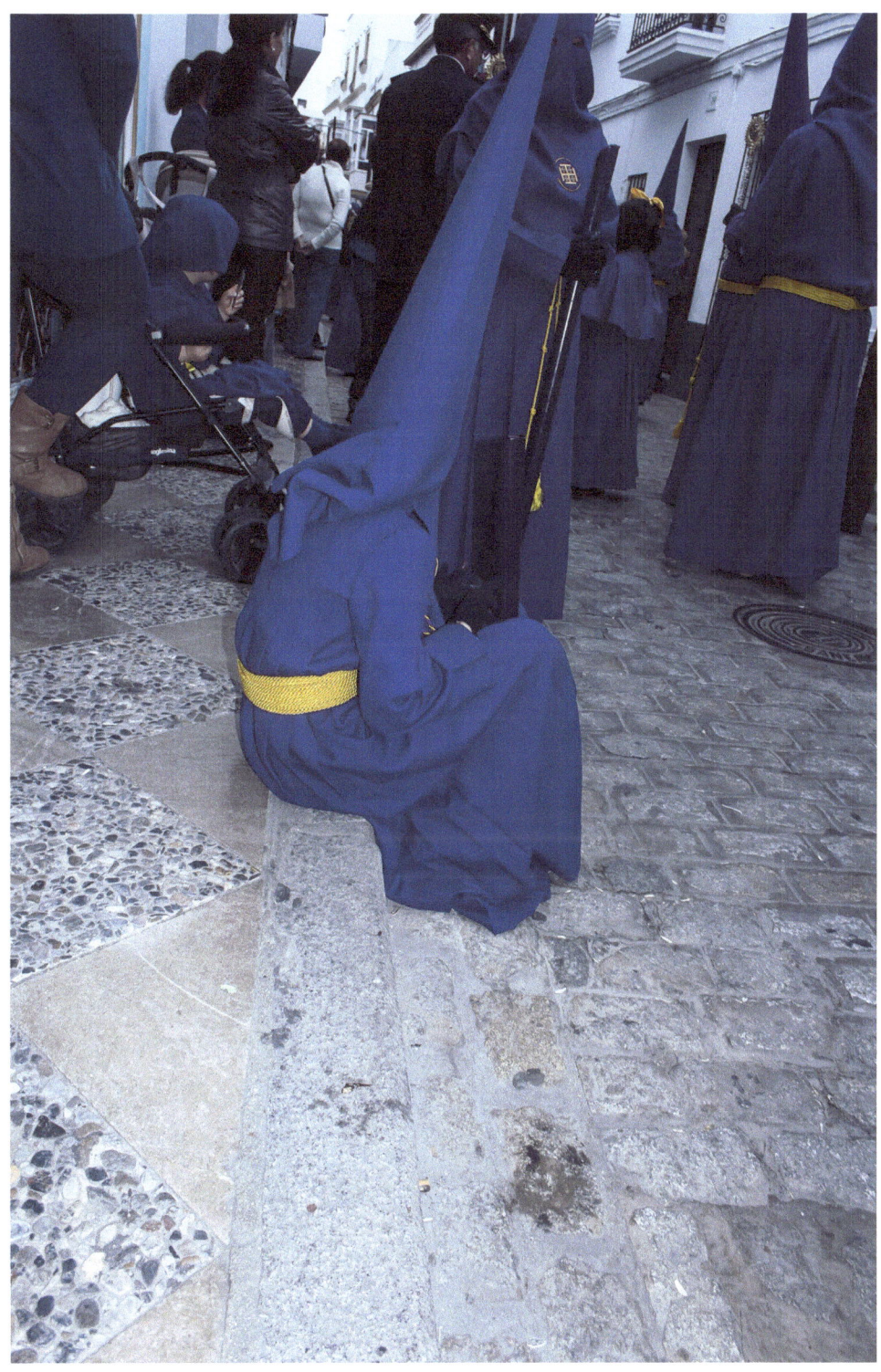

   This young man just had to take a break about half way through the Procession. It didn't dawn on me until later that he was ashamed of having to sit down and there I was recording it with my camera. I wish I could have found him later and told him how proud I was of him for doing such a noble thing.

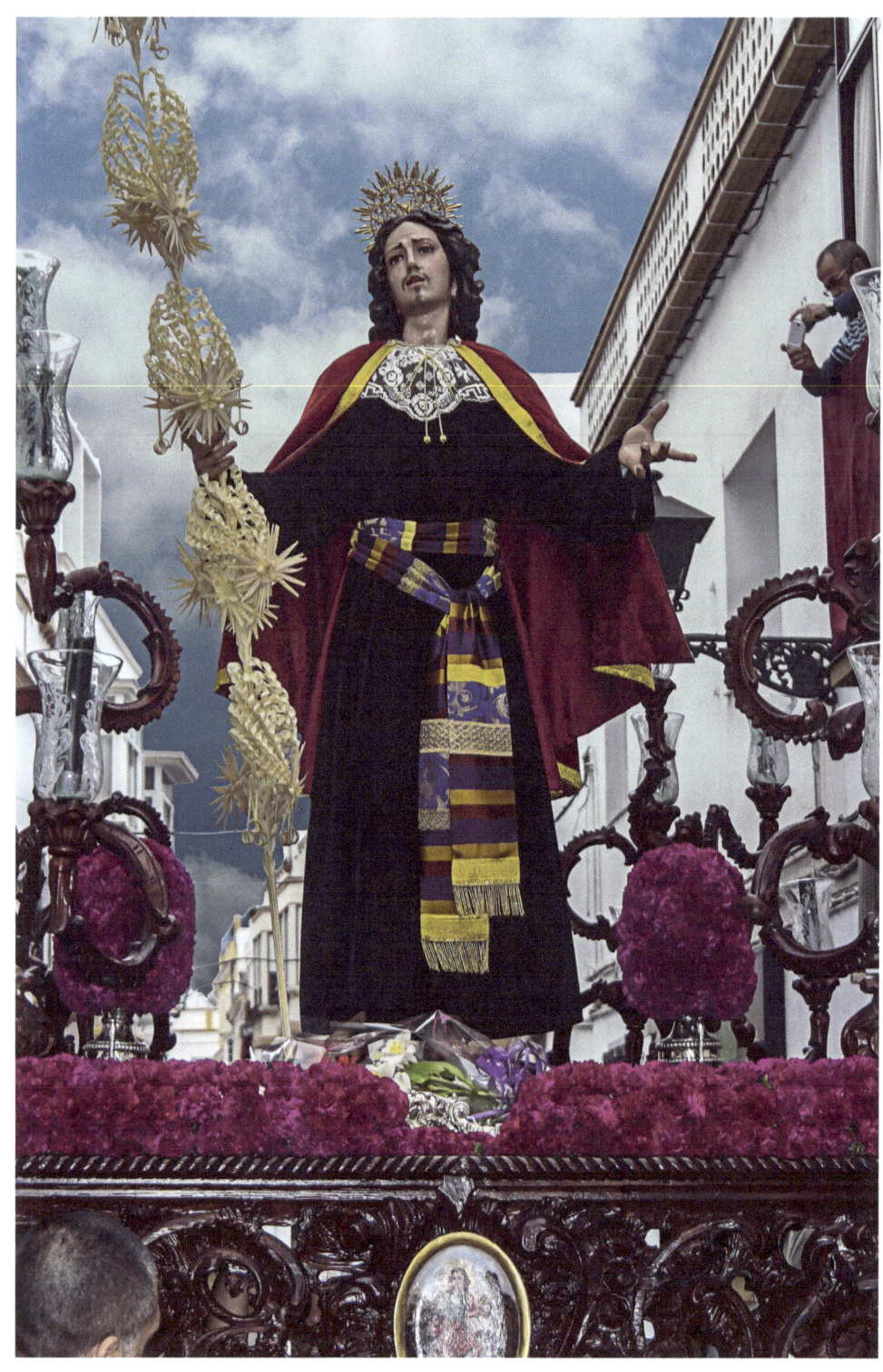

Float of Christ resurrected. I can only imagine the effect these floats and ceremonies had on people in the 16th century. They have a powerful effect on contemporary spectators so I'm sure the effect was staggering then. If you look closely you can see body parts of some of the Costaleros and get an idea of how confining it is and how little visibility they have on this type of float.

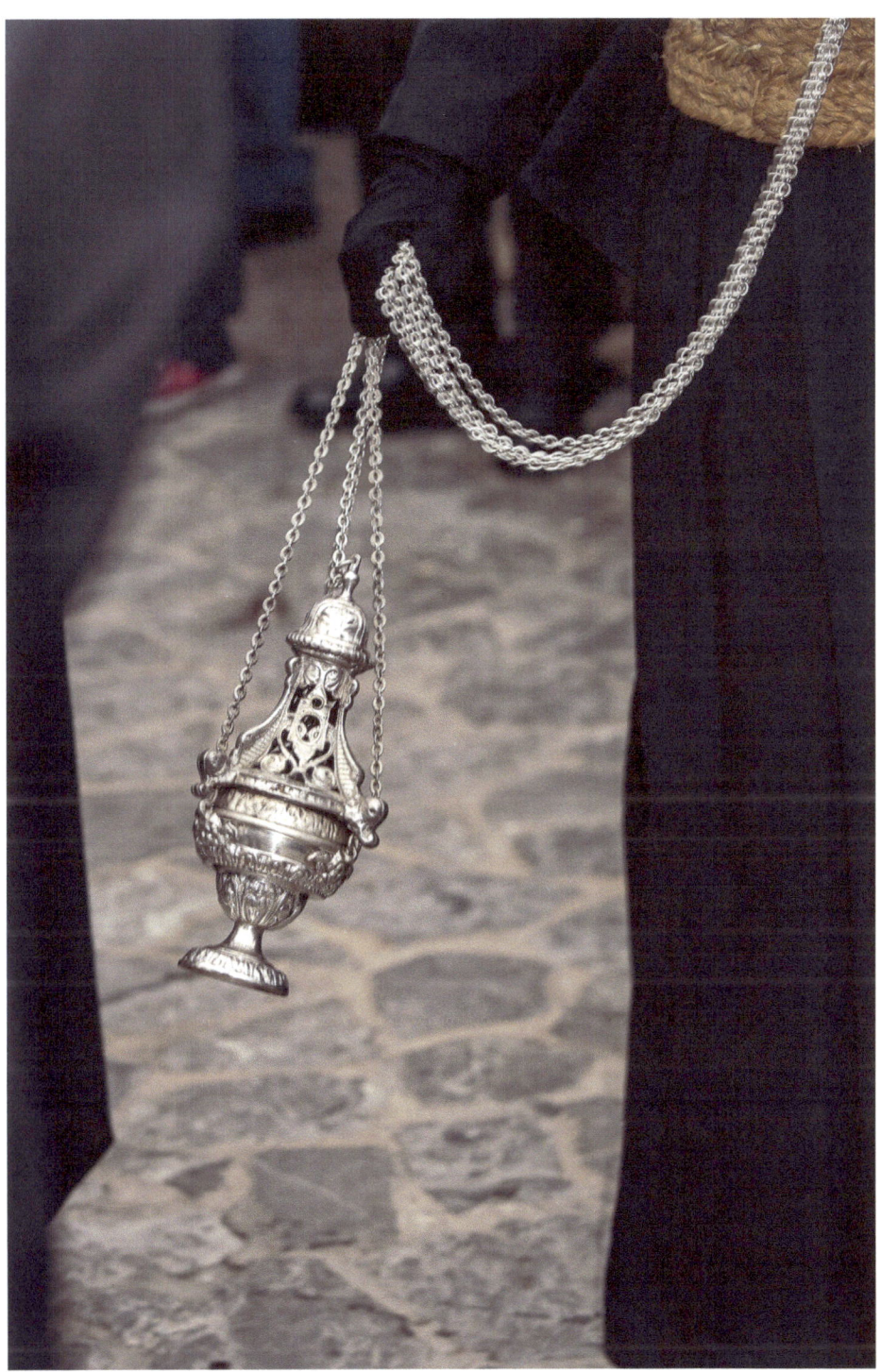

   I was more focused on the little pieces that go into a Procession here and the above is called a Thurible. They burn charcoal in it and put incense on top of it to smoke things up and bring that distinctive smell to the ceremony. To say all of the senses (sight, hearing, smell, touch, and taste) are stimulated would be understatement. They are fully submerged into a spectacle of sensory extravagance.

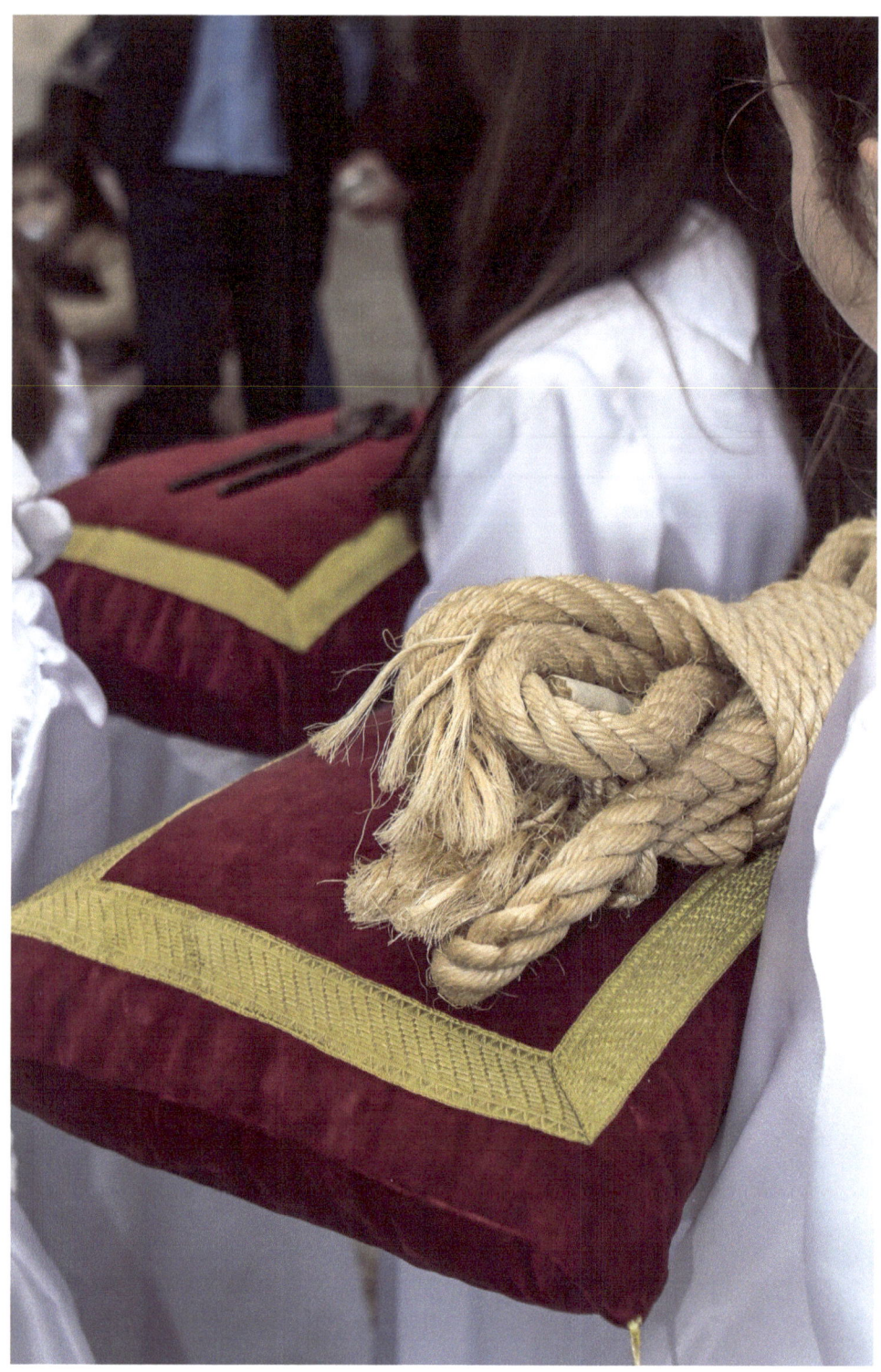

Here are replicas of the Pincer and Cord used to remove and lower Christ from the Cross. I photographed a replica of the Holy Lance also but those shots were not good enough to make it into the book. I only mention it to suggest the amount of detail that goes into these events.

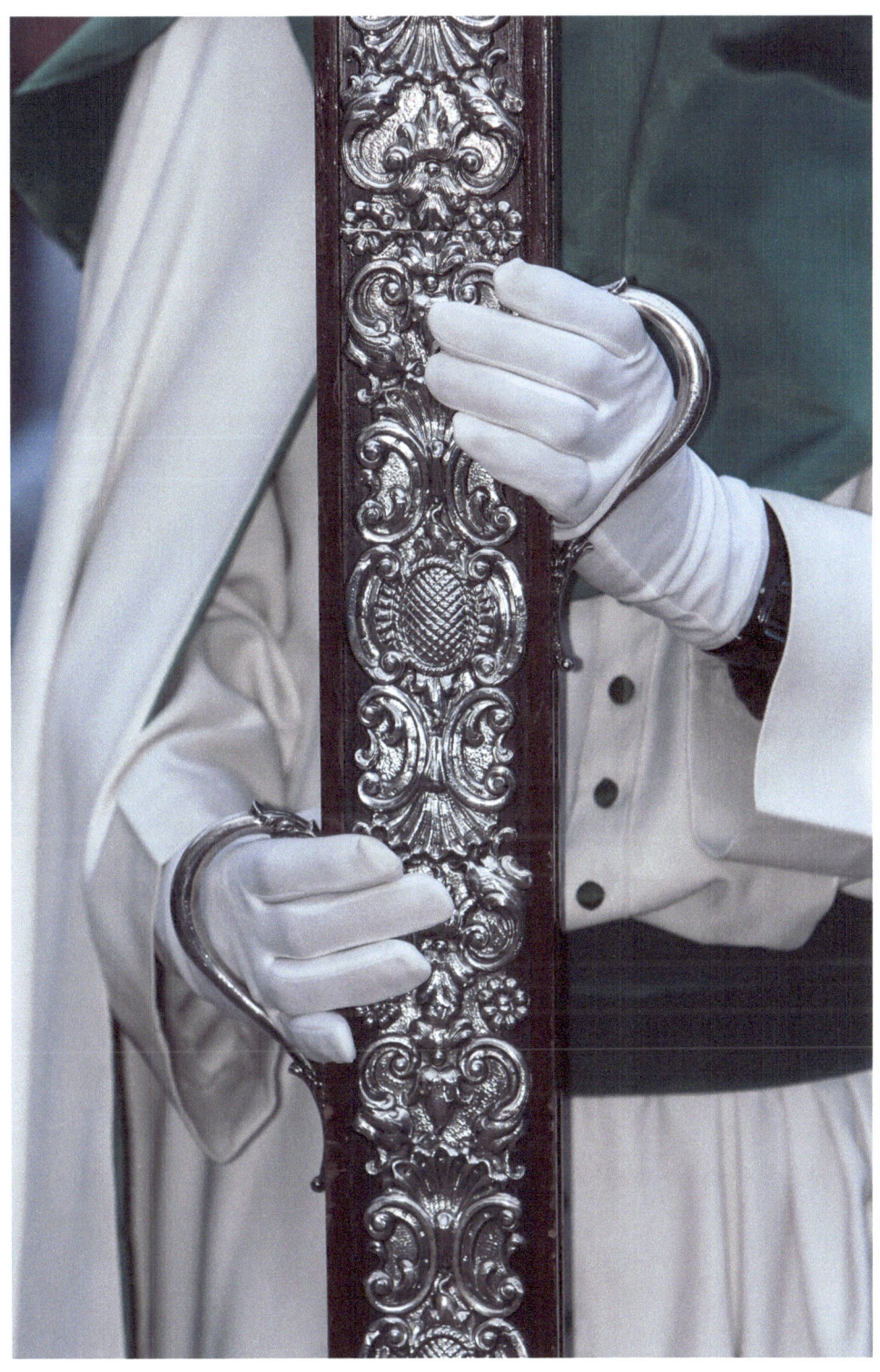

Close detail of the handles of the Guiding Cross. On Holy Tuesday while I was in El Puerto de Santa Maria visiting one of the Brotherhoods I was allowed to lift their Guiding Cross and I would guess that it had to weigh at least 30 lbs, probably more.

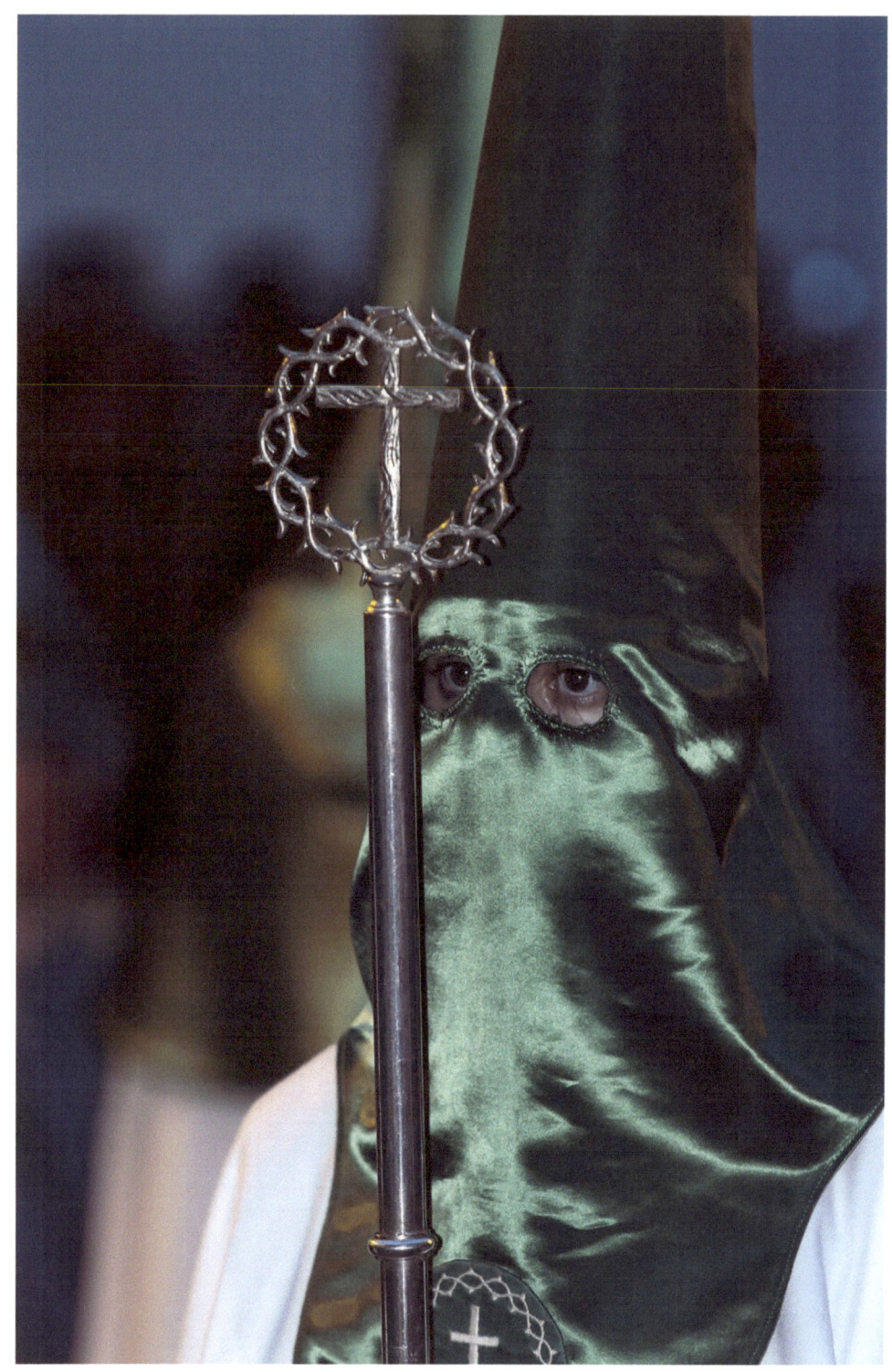

Penitent and staff. What caught my eye here is the abstract circle of fish surrounding the Crucifix on this otherwise very austere staff. You can see the Brotherhood's badge on his Capirote is a near perfect reflection of the ornament on the staff although I would not have gotten the fish abstraction had I not seen the staff.

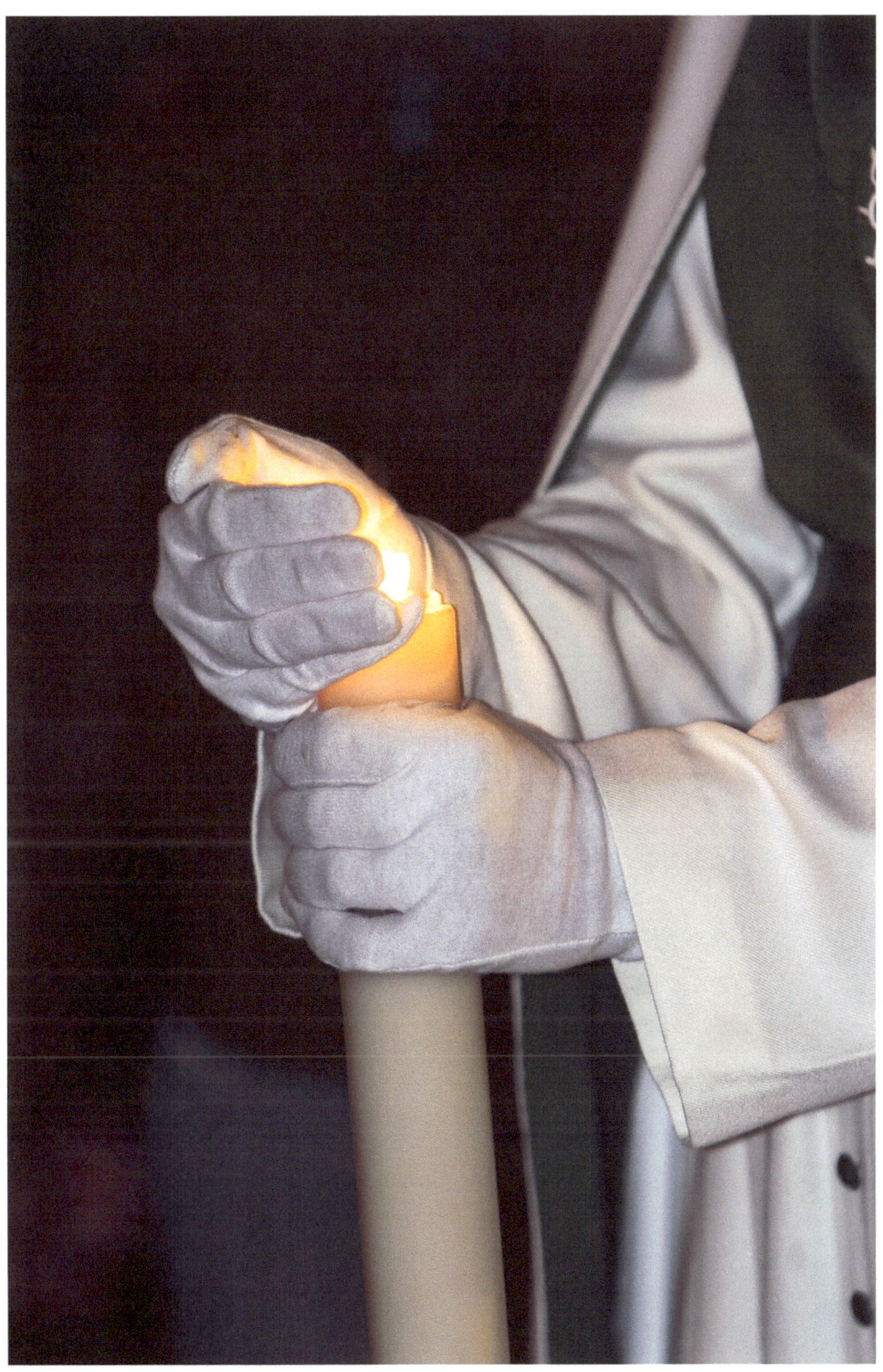

Keeping the flames burning. It seemed everyone had something unique to do with their candle. Some would let them burn only on one side thus creating a long trough along the candle. Others would let the wax drip in such a way that trails of wax would be hanging off the candle like icicles from a roof. Still others liked to get wax all over their gloves. I think they just needed something to do.

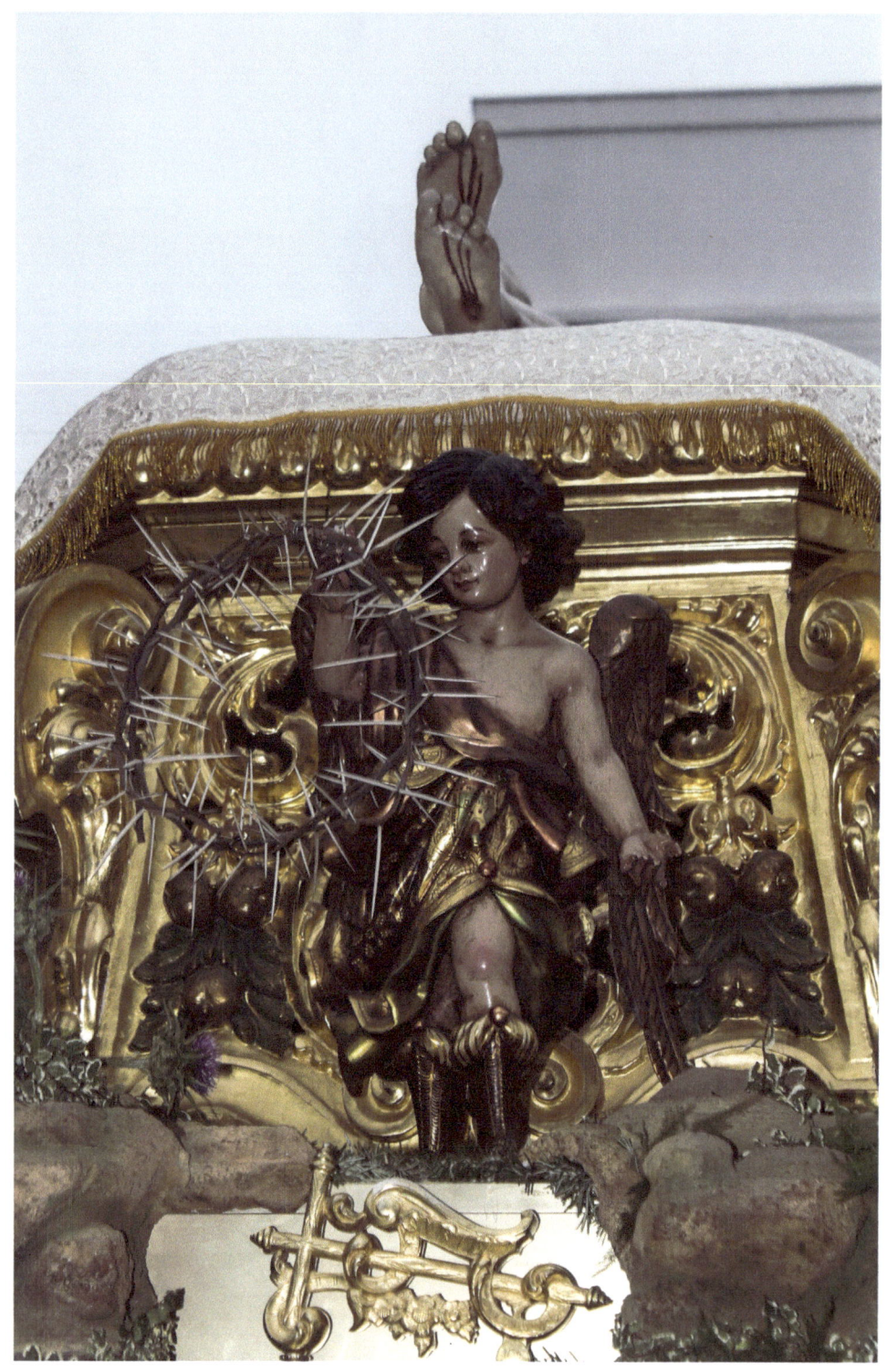

The bloody feet of Christ above an Angel holding his Crown of Thorns. That is gold plating over what I believe is wood and if that is the case, there has to be an awful lot of maintenance done on these floats. Also consider that many of these floats are hundreds of years old.

Domingo de Resurrección (Easter Sunday)

   Due to the age and value of the Pasos (floats) if it is raining at all the Procession gets canceled. This was the case throughout most of the Cadiz providence this year (2014) and there were no Processions I could find to attend within a reasonable driving distance. My hope is to update this book periodically as I learn more about Spanish Processional ceremonies and return there from time to time.

In Closing

This has been one of the most gratifying projects I have ever done both on a professional and spiritual level. Clearly, I have high hopes for the success of my first book but if it doesn't attract a large audience I am still very proud of the lucid, cohesive statement I have been able to accomplish in so few pictures.

As I have alluded to in the text above, I hope to update this book from time to time in order to make it more compelling. Also, if you are interested in viewing these pictures on a larger scale, go to fineartamerica.com and search on my name and you will find a good number of the pictures in this book posted there along with other pieces of my works. They are also available for purchase through Fine Art America should you so desire.

I encourage you to also visit http://douglomanphotography.com where you will find my Limited Edition Fine Art prints. My Limited Edition prints are of the highest quality and printed on aluminum and limited to 99 copies whereupon the file will be forever retired. The shot of the float of the Crucifixion with the full moon rising in the background will be found there. Contact me through the website for pricing on Limited Edition Prints.

By all means, like the Doug Loman Photography Facebook page as it is a great way to keep up with what I am doing and working on. I am already well on my way to publishing a book about Pictured Rocks National Lakeshore and I have many ideas on what to do after that but I haven't yet made a decision as to which one will be next.

I want to thank you for purchasing this book and if you enjoyed it could you be so kind as to leave a review of it on Amazon? I will be forever grateful.

About the Author

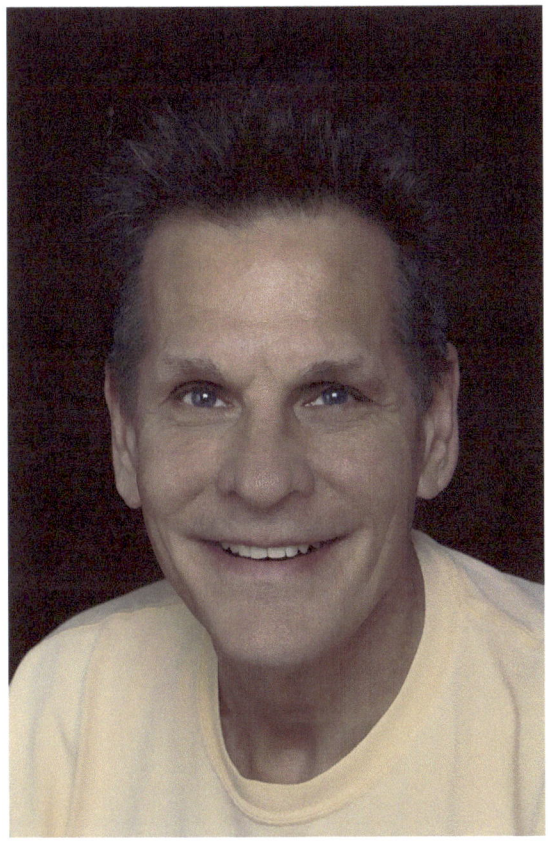

Doug Loman resides in Southeastern Wisconsin with his wife Lynn. When he is not out looking for the next great landscape he is usually playing with his Grandchildren.

www.ingramcontent.com/pod-product-compliance
Lightning Source LLC
Chambersburg PA
CBHW040748200526
45159CB00023B/1796